Messiah's Alphabet

Book 1

A workbook for learning how to read, write and pronounce the letters of the Hebrew alphabet

Messiah's Alphabet

Book 1

A workbook for learning how to read, write and pronounce the letters of the Hebrew alphabet

James T. and Lisa M. Cummins

Messiah's Alphabet Book 1:
A workbook for learning how to read, write and pronounce the letters of the Hebrew alphabet
Copyright © 2014 by James T. and Lisa M. Cummins
First printing 2014

Published by James T. and Lisa M. Cummins
Lady Lake, Florida 32159 USA

This publication may be freely reproduced in hardcopy on paper, in whole or in part, by any individual or organization, provided that (a) the contents are not altered in any way and (b) any resulting electronic or paper reproductions are never sold or made available to others in exchange for payment of any kind.

Interior design by Lisa M. Cummins

Cover design by Lisa M. Cummins

Printed in the United States of America

For Owen.

———————————

*Thanks to the Beginner's Hebrew class
of Congregation Sh'ma Yisrael
for your suggestions and encouragement
which were of great help
in producing this book.*

———————————

Indeed, then I will return my people to a pure language
so that they all may call upon the name of the LORD,
serving him with a united will.
Zephaniah 3:9, ISV

Table of Contents

Introduction 9
Audio Files and Other Online Help 10
Helpful things to know about the Hebrew Alphabet 11
About Hebrew Consonants and Vowels 12
Meet the Hebrew Alphabet CHEAT SHEET! 13
Aleph-Bet and Vowels "CHEAT SHEET" 15
Aleph-Bet Writing Practice 17
Further Alphabet Practice 23
About Hebrew Nuggets 24
Hebrew Nugget: Yeshua 25
How to make syllables 26
Let's make syllables! 27
Transliteration on the Farm 29
More Syllable Practice 30
Hebrew Nugget: Mosheh 31
Double Syllables 32
Double Syllable Practice 33
Hebrew Nugget: Shalom 35
Masculine Nouns and Pronouns 36
Masculine Nouns and Pronouns Practice 37
More Nouns and Pronouns Practice 39
Feminine Nouns and Pronouns 40
Feminine Nouns and Pronouns Practice 41
"Me talk Hebrew pretty one day!" 43
Introducing Compound Vowels / Introducing Diphthongs 44
Hebrew Nugget: Elohim 46
Pronouns: Singular and Plural 47
Hebrew Nugget: Eretz 49
About Book Type 50
Book Type Flash Cards 51
The Furtive Patach 57
Hebrew Nugget: Mashiach 59
Hebrew Nugget: Ruach 60
Simple Sentences Using Pronouns and the "Top Ten" Nouns 61
Write Your Own Simple Sentences Using Pronouns and the "Top Ten" Nouns 63
The Definite Article 65
Hebrew Nugget: Echad 67
The Double-Duty Dot 68
The Double Sehgolet 69
Let's Read Scripture: The "Sh'ma" 70
For Further Study 71

Introduction

Welcome to your very first introduction to the Hebrew alphabet. We believe that, because you are holding this book in your hands, God has called you to begin to learn this wonderful Biblical language, and therefore it should be a rewarding, enjoyable, holy, and – yes – **fun** experience for you! Before we begin, let's offer together a prayer of thanksgiving to our Lord, Messiah **Yeshua** (that's Hebrew for "Jesus") for the chance to learn Hebrew. Amen!

This book was written for people who have never seen the Hebrew alphabet before. It is written in a "workbook" style so that you can practice writing the shapes of the letters. The goal is to help you learn to do four things:

1. **Read** the Hebrew letters (learn to recognize their shapes)
2. **Write** the Hebrew letters (learn to form their shapes)
3. **Speak** the Hebrew letters (learn to pronounce each letter)
4. **Understand** the Hebrew letters (learn basic Biblical words which we will introduce gradually).

As you begin to learn more about Hebrew, many wonderful new layers of meaning will begin to unfold from the scriptures. We know that almost the entire **TaNaCH** (Old Testament) was written in Hebrew, and some linguists believe much of the **B'rit Chadashah** (New Testament / Renewed Covenant) could have been originally written in Hebrew – and if not, it still is filled with Hebraic speech patterns arising from the culture of its mainly Jewish writers. Learning Hebrew, then, will help your understanding of scripture dramatically.

Some of you are Jewish believers in Yeshua, who will be using this book to prepare for your **Bar Mitzvah** or **Bat Mitzvah** (Son or Daughter of the Commandment) ceremony. We hope this book will serve you, not only to prepare for that wonderful day of "promise" to serve our Lord, but in the years to come as you continue in the study of His word.

> Indeed, then I will return my people to a pure language
> so that they all may call upon the name of the LORD,
> serving him with a united will.
> *Zephaniah 3:9, ISV*

> But the goal of our instruction is love from a pure heart
> and a good conscience and a sincere faith.
> *1 Timothy 1:5, NASB*

Audio Files and Other Online Help

If you will be studying this book on your own without the help of an instructor, we strongly suggest that you download the **FREE mp3 audio files** available on our website:

www.MessiahsAlphabet.com

The audio files will enable you to hear the correct pronunciation of the Hebrew letters. You will need an mp3 player, a computer, or other mp3-compatible device in order to listen to any files you choose to download. If you'd rather not download them, most web browsers are capable of playing these files "on screen."

In addition, this entire book is available in **pdf format as a FREE download.** Feel free to print as many copies as you need for your own practice or, if you are an instructor, for your students.

This book is copyrighted, but you may freely copy it as long as you agree to use the copies according to the following rules:

1) Don't change any of the content of the book, or re-use any of its content within the content of any other publication, electronic or otherwise. (Brief excerpts may be used in book reviews, provided our book is fully cited).

2) Don't post the pdf on the internet or make it otherwise available to anyone else electronically. (Putting a link on your website which redirects people to our website downloads page is an acceptable alternative.)

3) Don't sell copies of this book or require payment of any kind for either the copies themselves or the use of the copies.

We offer this book as a free gift in ministry to God's precious people. Enjoy!

Helpful things to know about the Hebrew Alphabet

Don't worry about memorizing the facts below, or trying to learn all these things right now. These facts will be introduced very gradually to you over the coming lessons, and you will naturally learn them just by doing the practice. However, we know that some students like to get the "big picture" before they begin, so we have taken this opportunity to list a few basic facts about the Hebrew alphabet.

1. Hebrew is read and written from **right to left.** Not only are the *words* in a sentence written from right to left, but also *each letter within the word* is written from right to left. It's like a mirror image of how we read and write English.

2. Hebrew is a **phonetic** language. That means each letter represents a distinct sound.

3. There are only **22 consonants** in the Hebrew alphabet. These are the "large, noticeable shapes" you see in a Hebrew sentence that look like actual letters.

4. Above and below these "large shaped" consonants are **tiny dots and dashes.** This is how **vowels** are represented in Hebrew.

5. **No letters of the Hebrew alphabet are ever "joined together."** For example, in English, we have a form of our writing called "script," in which each letter is physically joined to the next letter in a word. This never happens in Hebrew.

6. There are **no capital letters** (upper case letters) in Hebrew. In other words, Hebrew only has one case (unlike English, which has an "upper" case and a "lower" case). However, some Hebrew letters do have a **special shape called a "final form"** when they appear at the end of a word.

7. Biblical Hebrew often uses the letters of the alphabet to represent **numbers,** by assigning a numerical value to each letter. In ancient times, Hebrew did not use special symbols for numbers as we do today. Modern Israelis, however, are very familiar with the same "Arabic" numeral system we English speakers use (1, 2, 3, etc.) and they use these numerals in daily life.

8. There are two main pronunciations of the Hebrew language: the *Ashkenazi* (**Ashkenazic,** originating from Germanic/Eastern European Jews) and the *Sephardi* (**Sephardic,** originating from Spanish Jews). In all universities and throughout Israel, the Sephardic pronunciation has been adopted, since it is generally believed this pronunciation is nearest to the original. In our lessons, we will be using the Sephardic.

9. "What about Yiddish? What's that?" **Yiddish** is actually a separate language used by Jews who lived in central and eastern Europe before the Holocaust. It was originally a German dialect blending words from Hebrew and other modern languages, and today it is still spoken (mainly in the US, Israel, and Russia). It will not be taught in this book.

About Hebrew Consonants and Vowels

This is a line from an English handwriting tablet:

In English, we would write the word "David" on it like this:

But Hebrew has no "upper case" distinction. The letters all basically have the same height:

"David" in Hebrew

Most letters stay between the lines:

Some rise above the top line a little. These are called "ascenders."

Some fall below the bottom line. These are called "descenders."

Vowels usually stay below the line under a consonant. (The "X" at right represents some Hebrew consonant.)

There are some exceptions. Sometimes a vowel might appear above or next to a consonant:

In Hebrew, letters are never joined. It is like English *print* lettering, which is not joined.

English script: "joined"   *English print: not "joined"*   *Hebrew: not "joined"*

People just beginning to learn English will write it in simplified block print. Books, though, are typed in fancier fonts called "book type." The same thing is true in Hebrew. This book will teach you to write the simplified block print.

English simplified block print   *English book type*   *Hebrew simplified block print*   *Hebrew book type*

Meet the Hebrew Alphabet
CHEAT SHEET!

On the following pages, you will find one page containing ALL the consonants and vowels of the Hebrew alphabet. Since this page contains EVERYTHING you will ever need to know to be able to sound out any Hebrew word, we have called this page the **CHEAT SHEET.**

Are you allowed to cheat in Hebrew? Yes, you are, and we encourage you to do so in this book!

Take a moment right now to gently tear out or cut out the CHEAT SHEET on page 15. You will want to have this sheet handy whenever you are doing your lessons. Fold it up if you like, and use it as your "bookmark" as you go through the book. That way, you won't have to flip through the book in case you forget a letter's name or how it is pronounced!

Also included in your workbook are some **Writing Practice** pages. They follow immediately after the Cheat Sheet, and they have dotted lines so you can practice writing the letters correctly. Once you have filled in all the available spaces, continue practicing writing the letters on regular lined notebook paper. **We suggest you spend several weeks practicing writing all the letters.** Try to write them daily if you can.

If you have an instructor, listen carefully as he or she pronounces each letter name and its sound. He or she will show you how to form each letter as you fill in your Writing Practice pages.

If you don't have an instructor, here's how to use the Cheat Sheet:

1. **Ignore the "Book Type" column for now.** Notice the name of each letter, the shape of each letter (in the Hand-Written column), and the "Sounds Like" column. **Practice writing the letters as you see them in the Hand-Written column by writing them out on the Writing Practice pages.**

2. Pay close attention to whether each letter **stays between the dotted lines, goes above the lines, or dips below the lines.** These features might be the only thing differentiating one letter shape from another. The same thing goes for letters which have **little pieces sticking out to the left or right side**, which we call a "**tail.**"

3. **Note that there is no "ch" sound in Hebrew as in "church" or "chip."** Any time you see a "ch" throughout this book (or any writings related to Hebrew), it is pronounced "**ch**" as in the German name "**Bach**" or the Scottish "**Loch** Ness." It's like pronouncing the sound for "h" with the back of your throat a little tightened to make it come out rough.

4. The **difference between a letter's NAME and what it SOUNDS LIKE** is best described by the following example. Let's say you wanted to tell your buddy how to spell the word "wig." You would tell him the NAME of each letter in order, saying this: "double-yoo" "eye" and "jee." These are the NAMES of the letters, but they aren't necessarily what they SOUND LIKE in the word "wig." What they actually SOUND LIKE is "wh," "ih" and

Meet the "Cheat Sheet", continued...

"gh". So, the **SOUNDS LIKE column** tells you how you should **PRONOUNCE** that letter within a Hebrew word.

5. Notice that some of the letters, like BAYT/VAYT (#2), seem to **change their names slightly** depending on changes in their forms. BAYT and VAYT are still considered to be "the same letter," but are really just different forms of that letter. (An example from English is that we have something we call a "capital **A**" and something we call a "lower case **a**" but we consider them to be the same letter, the letter A.) The presence of a "dot" in the center of a letter (called a **dagesh**) often "hardens" a letter's sound; the absence of a dot often "softens" it. The letters which change sounds when a dagesh is present are: BAYT/VAYT (#2), KAF/CHAF (#11), PAY/and FAY (#17). SHEEN/SEEN (#21) changes sound depending on whether the dagesh is on the right or the left side of the letter. TAHV (#22) keeps the same sound, whether the dagesh is present or absent.

6. Some letters change forms only when they appear at the **end of a word**; these special forms are called **"final forms."** The five letters which have final forms are: CHAF (#11), MAYM (#13), NOON (#14), PAY/FAY (#17) and TSADEE (#18).

7. Some letters have the same sounds as each other. We call them **"sound alike" letters.** Some examples are CHAYT (#8) and CHAF (#11b) or TAYT (#9) and TAHV (#22). In English, we often have the same situation: in the word "incense," for example, both the "c" and the "s" sound alike. In the word "francophile," the "f" and the "ph" sound alike.

8. About transliteration: **transliteration** means to take the letters of a foreign alphabet and write them in letters of your own familiar alphabet so that anyone who speaks your language can "sound out" the word. **Note: There are no spelling rules governing transliteration!** Any way you can spell it in English to get it pronounced correctly is acceptable. That's why there seems to be such a variety of English spellings for the same Hebrew word. For example, let's look at the following Hebrew word:

אֱלֹהֵינוּ

Assuming we don't know anything about these Hebrew letters, we'll need a **transliteration** to help us pronounce the word. Here are a few different **transliterations** of this word which would all be perfectly acceptable:

        eh-lo-hay-noo   elloheynu   elohaynu   ell-o-hay-nu

You see that there are no rules for how to spell transliterations. They are merely there to help you pronounce a word correctly. The other thing about transliterations is that **they don't provide any meaning.** To find the **meaning**, you would need a **translation**. (The translation of the Hebrew word above, by the way, is "our God.")

Since the names of the letters in our Cheat Sheet are just our own **transliterations** (we made up all these spellings), you will probably notice a wide variety of different spellings used in other books, including those used in your Bible.

ALEPH-BET and VOWELS "CHEAT SHEET"

	Book Type	Name	Sounds Like...	Hand-Written
1	א	Ah-lehf	*silent*	א
2(a)	בּ	Bayt	B as in Boy	בּ
2(b)	ב	Vayt	V as in Vase	ב
3	ג	Gih-mel	G as in Girl	ג
4	ד	Dah-let	D as in Door	ד
5	ה	Hay	H as in Hay	ה
6	ו	Vav	V as in Vase	ו
7	ז	Zah-yin	Z as in Zoo	ז
8	ח	Chayt	Ch as in Bach	ח
9	ט	Tayt	T as in Toe	ט
10	י	Yood, Yōd	Y as in Yarn	י
11(a)	כּ	Kaf	K as in Kite	כּ
11(b)	כ	Chaf	Ch as in Bach	כ
11(c)	ך	final Chaf	Ch as in Bach	ך
12	ל	Lah-med	L as in Light	ל
13(a)	מ	Maym	M as in Mom	מ
13(b)	ם	Final Maym	M as in Mom	ם
14(a)	נ	Noon	N as in Nose	נ
14(b)	ן	Final Noon	N as in Nose	ן
15	ס	Sah-mech	S as in Soup	ס
16	ע	Ah-yin	*silent*	ע

	Book Type	Name	Sounds Like...	Hand-Written
17(a)	פּ	Pay	P as in Pad	פּ
17(b)	פ	Fay	F as in Food	פ
17(c)	ף	Final Fay	F as in Food	ף
18(a)	צ	Tsah-dēē	TS as in Cats	צ
18(b)	ץ	Final Tsah-dēē	TS as in Cats	ץ
19	ק	Kōf	K as in Kite	ק
20	ר	Raysh	R as in Rope	ר
21(a)	שׁ	Shēēn	SH as in Ship	שׁ
21(b)	שׂ	Sēēn	S as in Soup	שׂ
22(a)	תּ	Tahv	T as in Top	תּ
22(b)	ת	Tahv	T as in Top	ת

VOWELS				
1	ָ	Kah-matz	ah as in all	ָ
2	ַ	Pah-tach	ah as in far	ַ
3	ִ	Chēē-rēēk	ih as in fin	ִ
4	ִי	Chēē-rēēk Mah-lay	ee as machine	ִי
5	ֵ	Tsay-ray	ay as in day	ֵ
6	ֶ	Seh-gol	eh as in met	ֶ
7	ׁ or וֹ	Cholam (with or without vav)	oh as in no	ׁ or וֹ
8	וּ	Shoo-rook	oo as in noon	וּ
9	ֻ	Koobootz	oo as in noon	ֻ
10	ְ	Sh'vah (schwa)	' as in Mc'Mann, or "uh" as in tak<u>e</u>n	ְ

Messiah's Alphabet Book 1 | Page 15

Please carefully tear this page

out of your book

and keep it handy

as a guide for your lessons.

Aleph-Bet Writing Practice

Starting at the **right** side of your paper, fill in the blanks. The first one of each line is already done for you as an example.

Begin here.

	Handwritten
אa	
Aleph	Name
(silent)	Pronounced

	Handwritten
ב	
Bayt	Name
"b"	Pronounced

	Handwritten
ב	
Vayt	Name
"v"	Pronounced

	Handwritten
ג	
Gih-mel	Name
"g"	Pronounced

	Handwritten
ד	
Dah-let	Name
"d"	Pronounced

	Handwritten
ה	
Hay	Name
"h"	Pronounced

	Handwritten
ו	
Vav	Name
"v"	Pronounced

Aleph-Bet Writing Practice, continued

ז Handwritten
Zah-yin Name
"z" Pronounced

ח Handwritten
Chayt Name
"ch" Pronounced

ט Handwritten
Tayt Name
"t" Pronounced

י Handwritten
Yood Name
"y" Pronounced

כּ Handwritten
Kaf Name
"k" Pronounced

כ Handwritten
Chaf Name
"ch" Pronounced

ך Handwritten
final Chaf Name
"ch" Pronounced

Aleph-Bet Writing Practice, continued

ל	Handwritten
Lah-med	Name
"L"	Pronounced

מ	Handwritten
Maym	Name
"m"	Pronounced

ם	Handwritten
final Maym	Name
"m"	Pronounced

נ	Handwritten
Noon	Name
"n"	Pronounced

ן	Handwritten
final Noon	Name
"n"	Pronounced

ס	Handwritten
Sah-mech	Name
"s"	Pronounced

ע	Handwritten
Ah-yin	Name
silent	Pronounced

Aleph-Bet Writing Practice, continued

פּ	Handwritten
Pay	Name
"p"	Pronounced

פ	Handwritten
Fay	Name
"f"	Pronounced

ף	Handwritten
Final Fay	Name
"f"	Pronounced

צ	Handwritten
Tsah-dee	Name
"ts"	Pronounced

ץ	Handwritten
final Tsah-dee	Name
"ts"	Pronounced

ק	Handwritten
Kof	Name
"k"	Pronounced

ר	Handwritten
Raysh	Name
"r"	Pronounced

Aleph-Bet Writing Practice, continued

שׁ Handwritten
Sheen Name
"sh" Pronounced

שׂ Handwritten
Seen Name
"s" Pronounced

תּ Handwritten
Tahv Name
"t" Pronounced

ת Handwritten
Tahv Name
"t" Pronounced

ָ Handwritten
Kah-matz Name
"ah" Pronounced

ַ Handwritten
Pah-tach Name
"ah" Pronounced

ִ Handwritten
Chee-reek Name
"ih" Pronounced

Aleph-Bet Writing Practice, continued

ִ	Handwritten
Chee-reek Mah-lay	Name
"ee"	Pronounced

	Handwritten
Tsay-ray ֵ	Name
"ay"	Pronounced

	Handwritten
Seh-gol ֶ	Name
"eh"	Pronounced

	Handwritten
Cholam (with vav) וֹ	Name
"o"	Pronounced

	Handwritten
Shoo-rook וּ	Name
"oo"	Pronounced

	Handwritten
Koobootz ֻ	Name
"oo"	Pronounced

	Handwritten
Sh'vah ְ	Name
"uh" (ə) or hesitation	Pronounced

Messiah's Alphabet Book 1 | Page 22

Further Alphabet Practice

Exercise 1: Daily Writing Practice

Every day, on a clean sheet of lined notebook paper, write the date at the top of the page. Then write three copies of each letter on each line, saying the letter's **name** and what it **sounds like** out loud. If you need to consult your cheat sheet, please do. Keep the sheets in a folder or binder, and refer to them for encouragement as a reminder of how far you have come in your Hebrew studies. Ready for something even more challenging? Try to write as many letters as possible from memory, every day! When can you stop doing Daily Writing Practice? As soon as you can write the entire alphabet from memory and can recite each letter's name and what it sounds like.

Exercise 2: Alphabet Flash Cards

Obtain a pack of 3x5 index cards. On one side of each card, draw the shape of a Hebrew letter, and on the reverse, write the letter's **name** and what it **sounds like**. Shuffle the cards well, then quiz yourself. See if you can remember the name of each letter and what it sounds like, just by looking at the shape of the letter. What's really good about this method is the random order. It challenges your brain to have to recall the letters unexpectedly. It also helps you spot your weak areas. Any cards you seem to "miss" more frequently you can keep in a separate stack and spend more time on those.

Exercise 3: Alphabet Song

Make up a song to help you remember the letters of the alphabet in order, or sing the letters within a melody or a rap which already exists. We like to sing the Hebrew alphabet to the tune of Yankee Doodle Dandy. You can hear this song by downloading the mp3 file from our website (see page 10 for details).

About Hebrew Nuggets

We hope you have been enjoying getting to know the Hebrew letters better! Now it's time to introduce you to our **Hebrew Nuggets** series.

Each **Hebrew Nugget** is a special page that presents a brand new Hebrew word to you – one which can be found in the Bible. Hebrew Nuggets are interspersed throughout this book so that you can get a break from the regular lessons and have a time of spiritual refreshment by learning real Biblical words. They are a real treat! And, just as the name suggests, whenever we "mine" the original language of the Bible we will always unearth riches of understanding.

Even though you may not be all that familiar with the letters at this stage, you can still enjoy learning the words in our Nuggets series. All you have to do is trace the big letters with a marker, highlighter or colored pencil, and then we will explain how to sound out each syllable. We will also provide a brief explanation of what the word means.

Our first Nugget is a very important, very special and very holy word. See if you can guess what it means before you get to the bottom of the page!

HEBREW NUGGETS

HOW MUCH BETTER IT IS TO GET WISDOM THAN GOLD!
AND TO GET UNDERSTANDING IS TO BE CHOSEN ABOVE SILVER.

Proverbs 16:16

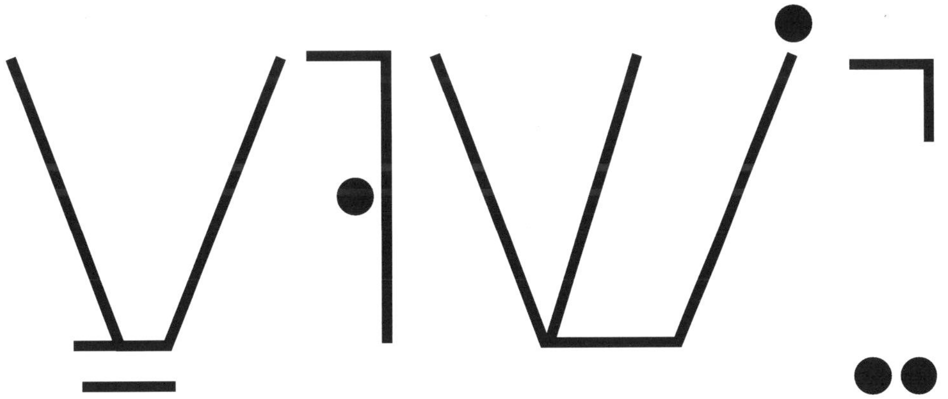

יְשׁוּעַ

right to left

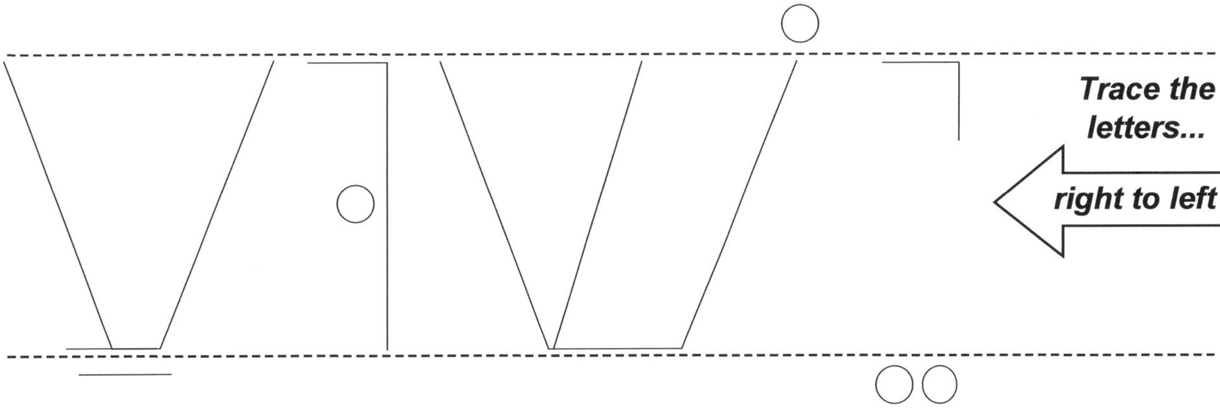

Trace the letters...

right to left

letter name:	**AH-YIN** and **PAH-TACH**	**SHEEN** **SHOO-ROOK**	**YOOD** and **TSAY-RAY**	*right to left, from top to bottom*
vowel name:				
consonant sound:	**(silent)**	**SH**	**Y**	*right to left, from top to bottom*
vowel sound:	**ah**	**oo**	**ay**	

transliteration (left to right): **yay-SHOO-ah**

English translation: means "he shall save," **Yeshua** (spelled as "Jeshua" in older translations in which the Latin J symbol was pronounced as the "y" sound); i.e., **Jesus.** Strong's #3442; this Hebrew word occurs 29 times in the TaNaCH (Old Testament Hebrew scriptures).

Messiah's Alphabet Book 1 | Page 25

How to make syllables

Well, you've been writing your alphabet every day, using your flash cards, and now you are ready to try to make syllables! Making syllables in Hebrew is pretty easy. Every syllable begins with a consonant, followed by a vowel. By combining the two together smoothly, you can create a syllable.

Example 1: Write the pronunciation (transliteration) for the following syllable:

Step 1: Start with the consonant MAYM, which is on TOP. (We always start at the TOP.) It is pronounced "m".
Step 2: Notice the vowel PATACH, at the BOTTOM. This is pronounced "ah".
Step 3: Smoothly blend the two sounds together: "m" + "ah" which gives us "mah."
Answer: "mah"

Example 2: Write the pronunciation (transliteration) for the following syllable:

Step 1: Starting at the top with the consonant AHYIN, we notice it is *silent*.
Step 2: The KAMATZ vowel below it is pronounced "ah."
Step 3: Blend the two sounds together: (silent) + "ah" which is simply "ah."
Answer: "ah" (*Now* you know why Hebrew has those funny silent consonants!)

Example 3: Write the pronunciation (transliteration) for the following syllable:

Step 1: Starting at the far RIGHT, we see a KOF, which is pronounced "K"
Step 2: The next item to the left is, believe it or not, a vowel (shoorook) pronounced "oo"
Step 3: Blend the two sounds together: "k" + "oo" which gives us "koo"
Answer: "koo"

Example 4: Write the pronunciation (transliteration) for the following syllable:

Step 1: Starting at the TOP, we see a SHEEN, which is pronounced "Sh"
Step 2: Underneath it is the vowel SH'VA, which is a "stop," "hesitation" or short "uh"
Step 3: Blend the two sounds together: "sh" + "uh" which gives us "shuh" or, better, "sh'"
Answer: sh'
(This syllable is used in the Sh'ma liturgy in the synagogue, Dt. 6:4, Mk 12:29)

Let's make syllables!

Use your cheat sheet to look up each consonant and vowel pair shown. "Transliterate" (write out the pronunciation for) each syllable in the space provided. The first three are done for you as an example. The answer key is on the back of this page.

bay ּבֵ **1**	may מֵ **2**	mah מָ **3**
___ בֵ **4**	___ גְ **5**	___ זָ **6**
___ הֱ **7**	___ זָ **8**	___ זֱ **9**
___ יֱ **10**	___ בָ **11**	___ חוֹ **12**
___ סֹף **13**	___ כְ **14**	___ לֱ **15**
___ נֹף **16**	___ טִ **17**	___ עָ **18**
___ פֵ **19**	___ פֱ **20**	___ צ **21**
___ קֹף **22**	___ רֱ **23**	___ שִׁ **24**

Messiah's Alphabet Book 1 | Page 27

Let's make syllables!

ANSWER KEY

3. מָ _mah_	2. מֵ _may_	1. בֵּ _bay_
6. דִ _dih_	5. גֶ _geh_	4. בֵ _vay_
9. ז _z'_	8. וָ _vah_	7. הֻ _hoo_
12. חוֹ _cho*_	11. טַ _tah_	10. יֵ _yay_
15. לֶ _leh_	14. כָ _chah*_	13. כוּ _koo_
18. עַ _ah_	17. סִ _sih_	16. נוּ _noo_
21. צ _tsah_	20. פֵ _fay_	19. פֶּ _peh_
24. שְ _sh'_	23. רוּ _roo_	22. קוּ _koo_

*Remember: "ch" in Hebrew is *always* pronounced like a rough-sounding "h" as in the names "Bach" or "Loch Ness." You should *never* pronounce it "ch" as in "church." That sound doesn't exist in Hebrew.

Messiah's Alphabet Book 1 | Page 28

Transliteration on the Farm

Did you know that, in Israel, even the animals speak Hebrew? (It's a little known fact). Match the animal to the sound the animal makes in Hebrew by drawing a line between the two columns. Also, write the transliterations in the blanks to the right. The first one is done for you.

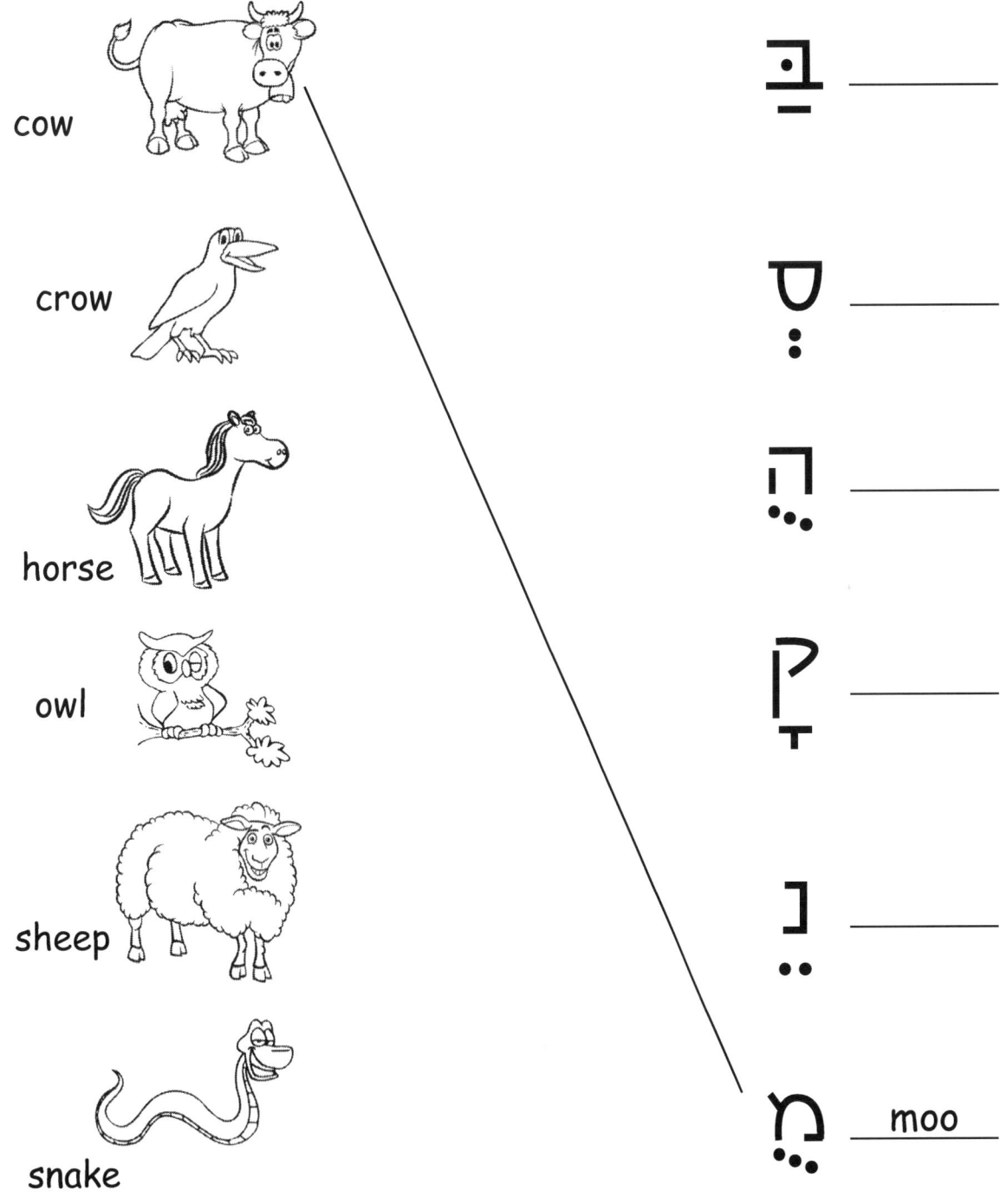

moo

More Syllable Practice

You'll need a lot more practice with syllables than our little workbook has given you. Here are a couple of creative ways to practice on your own.

Exercise: Use your flashcards to make random syllables.

Remember those flashcards you made with the Hebrew letters drawn on one side and the names/pronunciations on the other? Separate the deck of cards into two decks: Vowels and Consonants. Shuffle both decks.

Randomly choose one card from the consonant deck and one card from the vowel deck. On a sheet of lined notebook paper, write the consonant first, then the vowel either underneath or to the left, depending on where that vowel ordinarily appears. You've just created a syllable! Sound it out and write out the transliteration (pronunciation). Repeat process for as many syllables as you like.

Not challenging enough? Try this. Instead of writing anything down, hold the cards in the air in front of you, with the consonant on top and the vowel below (or to the left side, depending upon its usual placement). See how quickly you can vocalize each syllable, picking up a new pair of cards as soon as you finish the last pair. Time yourself with a timer to see how quickly you can get through the entire deck of consonants. (You'll need to re-use the vowel cards several times just to get through all the consonants.) Keep track of your best time and try to beat it.

Game: "Syllable War"

Remember the card game called "War"? Well, this is a card game you can play using your flashcards. You'll need a "study buddy" who is also going through this book with you and who has completed the lessons at least as far as this page.

One of you has the deck of vowel cards. The other has the deck of consonant cards. Each of you holds the cards under the table so you both can't see what either of you is holding. On the count of three, each person slaps one card from his deck on the center of the table, face up, so that you both can see the drawings of the consonant and the vowel. The two cards together will form a syllable. The first one who can shout out the syllable correctly gets a point. Put the cards back into their respective decks, reshuffle, and go again. The first one to get 10 points wins the game. (Warning: This game can get very loud. Have fun.)

HEBREW NUGGETS

HOW MUCH BETTER IT IS TO GET WISDOM THAN GOLD!
AND TO GET UNDERSTANDING IS TO BE CHOSEN ABOVE SILVER.

Proverbs 16:16

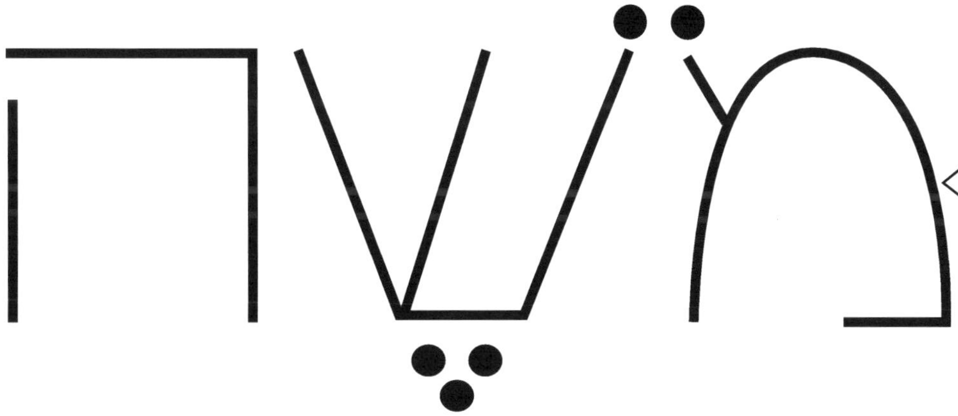

right to left

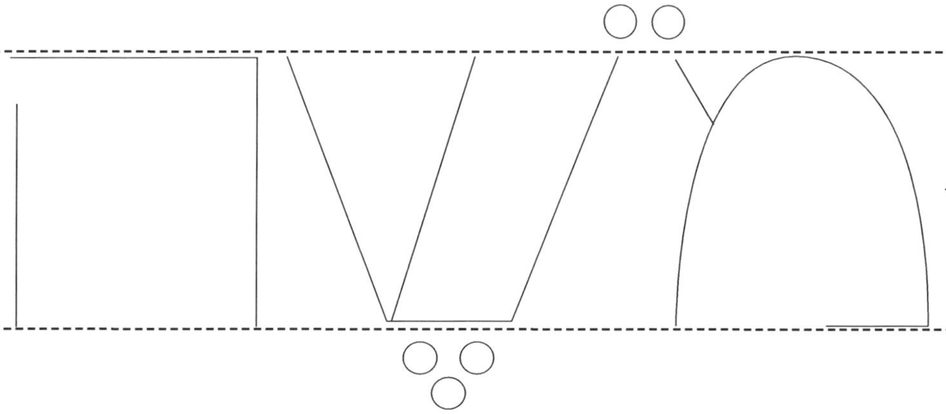

Trace the letters... right to left

letter name:	HAY	SHEEN and SEH-GOL	MAYM and CHOLAM	*right to left, from top to bottom*
consonant sound:	H (not actually pronounced)	SH	M	*right to left, from top to bottom*
vowel sound:		eh	oh	

transliteration (left to right): **mo - shěh**

English translation: **Moses (proper noun), a great leader and prophet of Israel.** The word's meaning, **"drawn out"** speaks of Moses being drawn out of the Nile as a baby hidden in a basket, as well as his calling to be used by God to "draw out" the people Israel from the land of Egypt. (Strong's #4872)

Messiah's Alphabet Book 1 | Page 31

Double Syllables

We've learned how to "sound out" syllables... single syllables, that is. What about words having more than one syllable?

It's not too hard to sound out words with two syllables. Just remember to begin at the **RIGHT** side of the word. Then, remember to start at the **TOP** of each syllable (the consonant) and then proceed to the vowel that is underneath it (or, occasionally, to the left of it). The diagram below shows the order in which you should read each Hebrew consonant and vowel (follow the numbers):

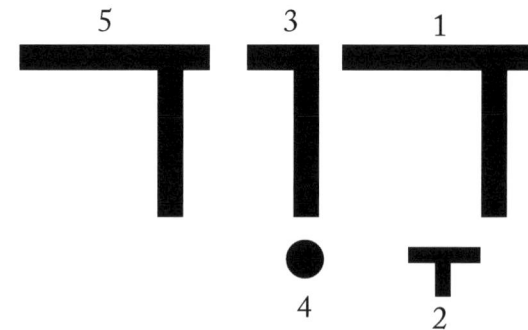

Now, let's follow the numbers and see what "sounds" come from each numbered item:

1	2	3	4	5	Transliteration: *Dah-vid*
d	ah	v	ih	d	Translation: David
dah		vid			

An easy way to remember the order is to tell yourself: RIGHT to LEFT, TOP to BOTTOM.

Now, you've probably noticed a few interesting things about the example above. One is that, even though we read Hebrew from *right to left*, our **transliterations** end up being written from *left to right*. This is because English is read from left to right, and we don't want to confuse anyone who will be reading our transliterations (including ourselves!) In the example above, we don't want to write our transliteration as "Vid-dah", because our readers who don't know Hebrew will mispronounce the word. When writing transliterations, we want to write them as if we were writing for a friend who doesn't know anything about the Hebrew alphabet, but who still desires to pronounce the words as correctly as possible. To make it easier on our friend, we would simply write, "Dah-vid."

The other thing you'll notice about this example is that sometimes a consonant gets "left hanging" all by itself at the end of a word, without any vowel under it. Whenever this happens, you pronounce the consonant as usual and just stop your voice, allowing that consonant to become the final sound of the syllable that came before it. (The last consonant simply becomes part of the syllable before it.)

Double Syllable Practice

Nonsense syllables: Use your cheat sheet to look up each consonant and vowel combination shown. "Transliterate" (write out the pronunciation for) each combination in the space provided. Remember to write your transliteration in the order that makes sense to the English reader -- that is, from left to right. The first three are done for you as an example. The answers are on the back.

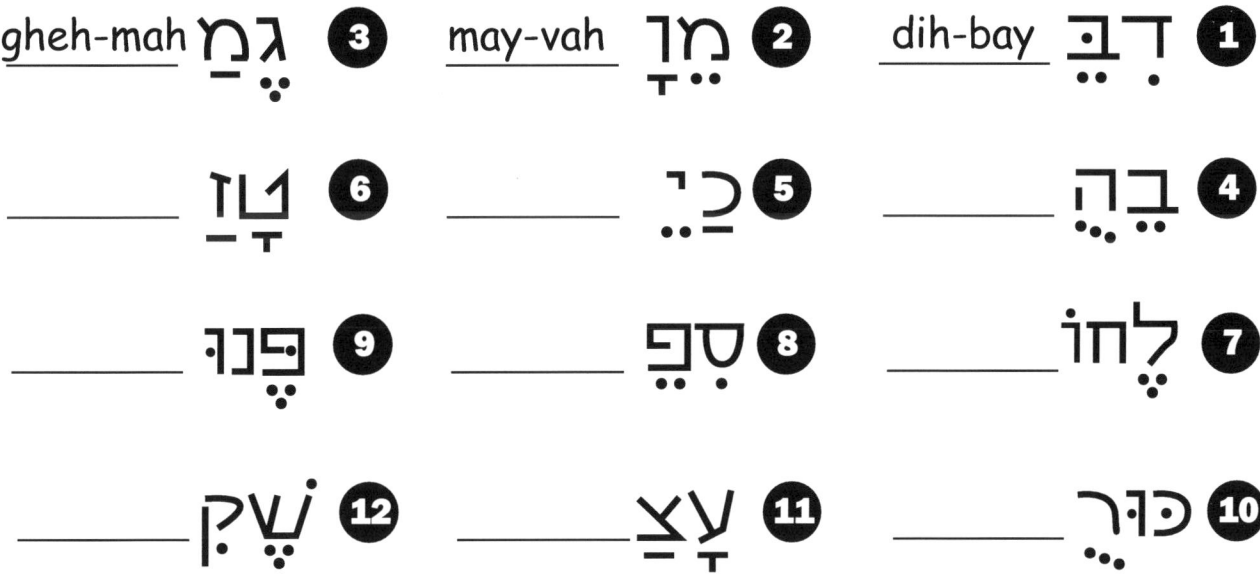

Real Words: Use your cheat sheet to look up each consonant and vowel combination shown. "Transliterate" (write out the pronunciation for) each syllable in the space provided. We have written the English meaning of each word next to it.

Double Syllable Practice

ANSWER KEY

1 דְּבֵי dih-bay   **2** מֵן may-vah   **3** גְּמָ gheh-mah

4 בֵהּ vay-hoo   **5** כִי chah-yay   **6** עַז tah-zah

7 לְחוֹ leh-cho   **8** סְפֵ sih-fay   **9** פֶנוּ peh-noo

10 כֻּרֵ koo-ray   **11** עַצָ ah-tsah   **12** שְׁקִ sheh-kih

13 שַׁבָּת shah-baht — *Sabbath*   **14** שָׁלוֹם shah-lohm — *peace*

15 לֶחֶם leh-chem — *bread*   **16** בָּרוּךְ bah-rooch — *blessed*

17 מֶלֶךְ meh-lech — *king*   **18** פְּרִי p'-ree — *fruit*

HEBREW NUGGETS

HOW MUCH BETTER IT IS TO GET WISDOM THAN GOLD!
AND TO GET UNDERSTANDING IS TO BE CHOSEN ABOVE SILVER.

Proverbs 16:16

שָׁלוֹם

← *right to left*

שָׁלוֹם

Trace the letters...

← *right to left*

letter name:	**FINAL MAYM**		**LAH-MED**		**SHEEN**	*right to left, from top to bottom*
vowel name:		**CHO-LAM (with VAV)**			**and KAH-MATS**	
consonant sound:	**M**		**L**		**SH**	*right to left, from top to bottom*
vowel sound:		**Ō**			**ăh**	

transliteration (left to right): **shă - LŌM**

English translation: **peace, prosperity, wholeness, completeness, well being, good health, soundness;** also used as a traditional greeting or blessing (Strong's #7965)

Messiah's Alphabet Book 1 | Page 35

Masculine Nouns and Pronouns

Now that you are reading double syllable words, you are ready to learn REAL Hebrew nouns and pronouns! You actually already learned a few in the last lesson!

A **noun** is a person, place or thing. A **pronoun** is a word that takes the place of a noun, referring to that noun.

About Hebrew gender: Unlike English, in Hebrew all words have a gender, either masculine or feminine. The reason we need to know the gender of a Hebrew word is to be able to add the correctly spelled suffixes to it (a skill which will become necessary later on in your studies).

NEW VOCABULARY FOR THIS LESSON:

	translation	transliteration	
nouns	father	ahv	אָב
	nation, people	ahm	עַם
	Israel	yis-rah-ayl	יִשְׂרָאֵל
	king	meh-lech	מֶלֶךְ
pronouns	he, it	hoo	הוּא
	this	zeh	זֶה
	you	ah-tah	אַתָּה

Masculine Nouns and Pronouns Practice

Masculine nouns and pronouns: Real Hebrew nouns and pronouns are listed below. **Transliterate** (write the pronunciation for) each word in the space provided. Also, write the **translation** (meaning) of each word in the space provided. The first exercise is done for you. The answers are on the back.

1. אָב — *transliteration:* ahv — *translation:* father
2. מֶלֶךְ — *transliteration:* ___ — *translation:* ___
3. עַם — *transliteration:* ___ — *translation:* ___
4. אַתָּה — *transliteration:* ___ — *translation:* ___
5. הוּא — *transliteration:* ___ — *translation:* ___
6. זֶה — *transliteration:* ___ — *translation:* ___
7. יִשְׂרָאֵל — *transliteration:* ___ — *translation:* ___

Simple noun sentences: Below, you will encounter your first actual Hebrew sentences. In Hebrew, the verb "to be" (such as *is, am, are, was,* and *were*) is often omitted from sentences. To translate these sentences into English, we often must insert the English verb "to be." Also, where necessary, we might need to add the indefinite article "a" or "an" into our English translation. For each noun sentence below, write its transliteration and translation. The first exercise is done for you.

8. הוּא מֶלֶךְ. — *transliteration:* Hoo meh-lech. — *translation:* He (is a) king.
9. זֶה יִשְׂרָאֵל. — *transliteration:* ___ — *translation:* ___
10. יִשְׂרָאֵל עַם. — *transliteration:* ___ — *translation:* ___
11. אַתָּה אָב. — *transliteration:* ___ — *translation:* ___

Masculine Nouns and Pronouns
ANSWER KEY

Masculine nouns and pronouns:

2	מֶלֶךְ	meh-lech	king	**1**	אָב	ahv	father
4	אַתָּה	ah-tah	you	**3**	עַם	ahm	nation, people
6	זֶה	zeh	this	**5**	הוּא	hoo	he, it
7	יִשְׂרָאֵל	yis-rah-ayl	Israel			

Simple noun sentences:

8 הוּא מֶלֶךְ. — Hoo meh-lech. — He (is a) king.

9 זֶה יִשְׂרָאֵל. — Zeh yis-rah-ayl. — This (is) Israel.

10 יִשְׂרָאֵל עַם. — Yis-rah-ayl ahm. — Israel (is a) people.

11 אַתָּה אָב. — Ah-tah ahv. — You (are a) father.

More Nouns & Pronouns Practice

Have you already finished the exercise on the previous page about Masculine Nouns and Pronouns? Very good! However, that one little exercise really is not enough practice for you to truly remember the meanings and spellings of all those new words. **It takes about 12 different repetitions of seeing, writing, speaking and hearing a new word before it becomes part of your memory.** Here's some additional practice which will really help:

Exercise: Write the vocabulary words daily for twelve days.

Every day for twelve days, **write** each Hebrew word onto a piece of notebook paper (you can copy it directly from the exercise pages). Next to it, write how it is pronounced (transliteration), then write what it means (translation). After writing each item, pause to **read** it again, then **speak** it aloud, and **listen** to your own pronunciation. This will involve your hands, sight, speech and hearing, which will help imprint the new word much more heavily into your memory. **(The more of your senses and muscles you involve in learning new material, the better you will remember the new material.)**

Exercise: Create flashcards and use them daily.

Probably the easiest way for some people to learn new vocabulary is to create a set of flashcards. On a new stack of 3x5 index cards, write the **Hebrew** word (in Hebrew characters only) on one side. On the other, write the **transliteration, translation**, and (this will become very important later), the **gender** (masculine, in this case). You might just write an "m" for masculine and an "f" for feminine. Quiz yourself daily with the cards. On Monday, look only at the Hebrew side and try to guess the pronunciation and meaning without looking at the back. (After you guess, turn the card over to see if you were right). Then, on Tuesday, look only at the translation/transliteration side of the card, and see if you can remember how to correctly spell the word in Hebrew. Alternate which side you look at each day. Make sure to shuffle the cards well to keep them random. Also, you should occasionally pull out the "problem cards" – the ones you keep missing – and do some extra practice with those. Afterward, shuffle them back into the deck and continue with random practice.

Bad at writing Hebrew characters? Several of our students felt like they were pretty bad at writing Hebrew at first. They were really worried about making their own flashcards because they were sure they would mess up the order of the letters, or forget a vowel. So, they just made photocopies of the words from the lessons in this book, then cut up the copies and taped them to blank 3x5 cards to create a very professional looking set of flashcards! They didn't have to worry about any spelling errors this way.

Flashcards make an excellent study method for learning ANY new subject, not just Hebrew vocabulary. You and your study buddy can quiz each other or make up games using your cards.

Feminine Nouns and Pronouns

You are now ready to learn some feminine nouns and pronouns. By the way, since we're talking about **gender**, it's important to realize that the **genders of Hebrew words can sometimes be very arbitrary.** In some cases, the assigned genders for certain words make perfect sense. A "father" will be masculine, and a "mother" will be feminine. Okay, that's pretty obvious. But in other cases, there seems to be no rhyme or reason. A "truth" is feminine, a "nation" is masculine, a "day" is masculine, a "sabbath" is feminine. Such gender assignments within the language must simply be memorized. Israeli children learn these things naturally as they are growing up and don't think much about it, but we English speakers must learn them by memory. Be sure to add the gender of each new word to your vocabulary lists or flashcards.

NEW VOCABULARY FOR THIS LESSON:

	translation	transliteration	
nouns	mother	aym	אֵם
	blessing	b' rah-chah	בְּרָכָה
	Sarah	sah-rah	שָׂרָה
	sabbath	shah-baht	שַׁבָּת
pronouns	you	aht	אַתְּ
	she	hee	הִיא
	this	zoht	זֹאת

Messiah's Alphabet Book 1 | Page 40

Feminine Nouns and Pronouns Practice

Feminine nouns and pronouns: Real Hebrew nouns and pronouns are listed below. Transliterate (write the pronunciation for) each word in the space provided. Also, write the **translation** (meaning) of each word in the space provided. The first exercise is done for you. The answers are on the back.

1 אֵם — aym — mother

2 שָׂרָה — _____ — _____

3 אֵת — _____ — _____

4 שַׁבָּת — _____ — _____

5 הִיא — _____ — _____

6 זֹאת — _____ — _____

7 בְּרָכָה — _____ — _____

Simple noun sentences: Below, you will encounter actual Hebrew sentences. In Hebrew, the verb "to be" (such as the words *is, am, are, was,* and *were*) is omitted from sentences. To translate these sentences into English, we often must insert the English verb "to be." Also, where necessary we might need to add the indefinite article "a" or "an" into our English translation. For each noun sentence below, write its transliteration and translation. The first exercise is done for you. Answers are on the back.

8 שָׂרָה אֵם. — Sah-rah aym. — Sarah (is a) mother.

9 הִיא שַׁבָּת. — _____ — _____

10 זֹאת בְּרָכָה. — _____ — _____

11 אֵת שָׂרָה. — _____ — _____

Messiah's Alphabet Book 1 | Page 41

Feminine Nouns and Pronouns Practice
ANSWER KEY

Feminine nouns and pronouns:

1. אֵם — aym — mother
2. שָׂרָה — sah-rah — Sarah
3. אַתְּ — aht — you
4. שַׁבָּת — shah-baht — sabbath
5. הִיא — hee — she
6. זֹאת — zoht — this
7. בְּרָכָה — b'rah-chah — blessing

Simple noun sentences:

8. שָׂרָה אֵם. — Sah-rah aym. — Sarah (is a) mother.
9. הִיא שַׁבָּת. — Hee shah-baht. — It (is a) sabbath.
10. זֹאת בְּרָכָה. — Zoht b'rah-chah. — This (is a) blessing.
11. אַתְּ שָׂרָה. — Aht sah-rah. — You (are) Sarah.

"Me talk Hebrew pretty one day!"

By now, you've had a little practice reading, writing and speaking simple Hebrew noun sentences. Interestingly, these noun sentences are made up of nothing but nouns! Reading some of these sentences in exact, literal order makes it sound like Tarzan is trying to do the translation:

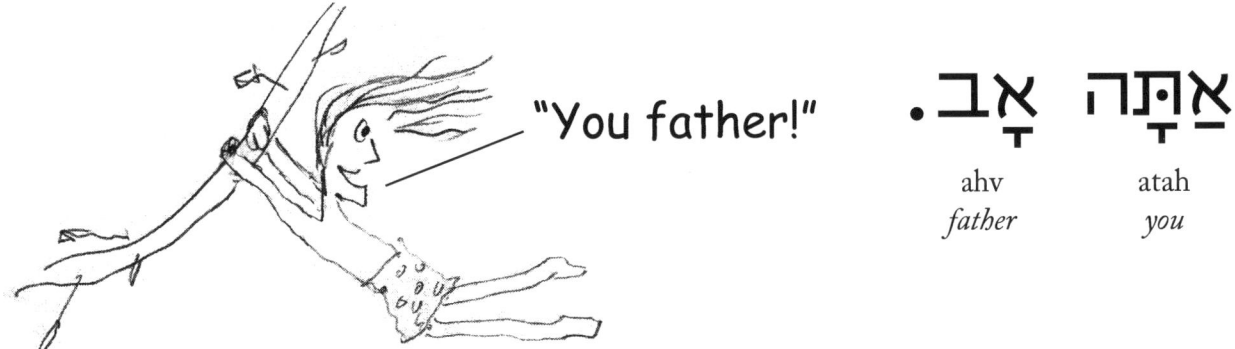

"You father!"

אַתָּה אָב.

ahv   atah
father   *you*

You've learned that you sometimes have to insert a verb (am, are, is) that isn't there in the text, but **is implied**. Also, you've sometimes had to insert an indefinite article ("a" or "an") that isn't there in the text. We like to joke that the literal Hebrew sounds like Tarzan, but the translation into English sounds like Jane *correcting* Tarzan:

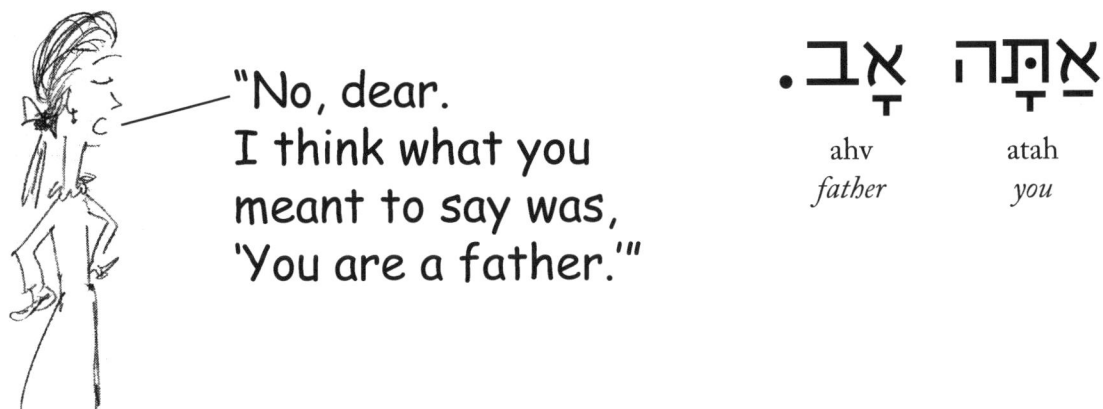

"No, dear. I think what you meant to say was, 'You are a father.'"

אַתָּה אָב.

ahv   atah
father   *you*

This requirement to add words to a translation is one of the reasons translators have such a tough job, especially Bible translators. This is also one of the reasons that no two translations of the Bible are the same. Translation is not an exact science, nor is it a "word for word" code where one word may automatically be inserted to replace another. It is much more of a "scholarly art." Thank God we have *Ruach ha Kodesh*, the Holy Spirit, who guides us into all truth and brings us the true sense of the Bible, even though most of us have to use translations to understand it.

Hope one day we talk Hebrew good, too.

Introducing Compound Vowels

In Hebrew, you will sometimes come across words in which two vowels are written right next to each other - both underneath the same consonant. We call these "**compound vowels.**" Usually, they involve the vowel **sh'va** (:) written together with another vowel. In olden days, this signalled a shortened vowel sound (called a Hataf vowel). In modern Hebrew, however, the sh'va is ignored and the other vowel is simply pronounced as usual. Write the transliteration of each nonsense syllable in the blanks below.

Introducing Diphthongs

A **diphthong** is defined as a sound formed by the combination of two vowel sounds. Examples in English are the vowel sounds in "coin" and "loud." The consonant "y" may also be used to create diphthongs. For example, "a" + "y" = "ay". Note the difference the "y" makes in pronouncing the word "ma" and the word "may." Another example is "so" and "soy". It's as if we begin pronouncing the vowel as usual and then blend our voices toward an "ee" to create the diphthong sound. Hebrew uses the **yod** in the same manner. Whenever it directly follows another vowel, the voice blends the vowel toward an "ee" sound to often create an entirely new vowel sound. You've already experienced this with the **chiriq mah-lay**.

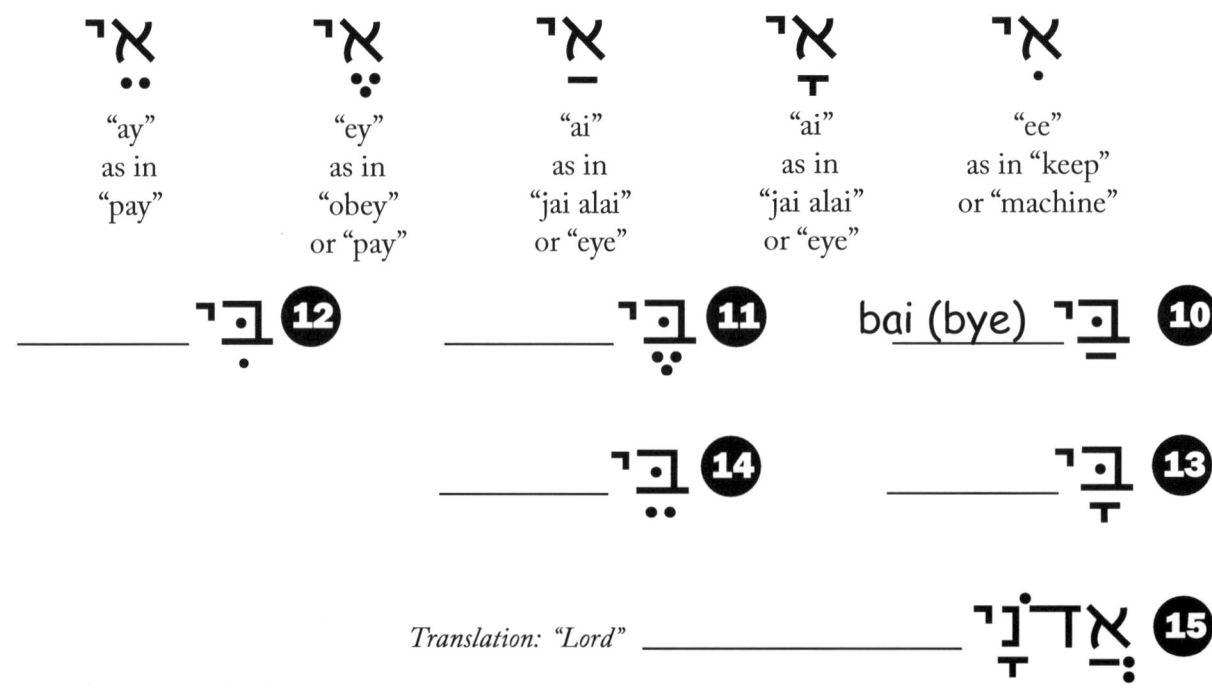

Translation: "Lord"

Introducing Compound Vowels

ANSWER KEY:

meh ﬦָ ③	beh בֱ ②	eh אֱ ①
dah דָ ⑥	gah גָ ⑤	ah אָ ④
zah זֲ ⑨	vah וֲ ⑧	ah אֲ ⑦

Introducing Diphthongs

ANSWER KEY:

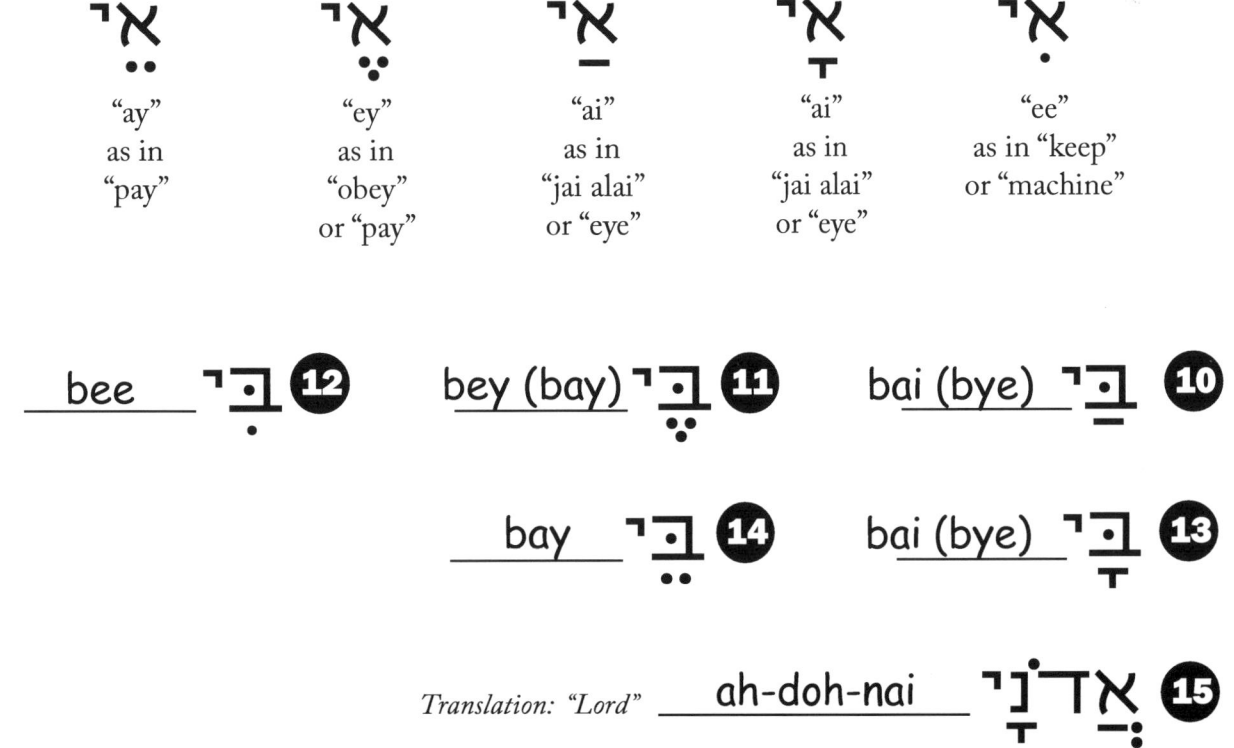

HEBREW NUGGETS

HOW MUCH BETTER IT IS TO GET WISDOM THAN GOLD!
AND TO GET UNDERSTANDING IS TO BE CHOSEN ABOVE SILVER.

Proverbs 16:16

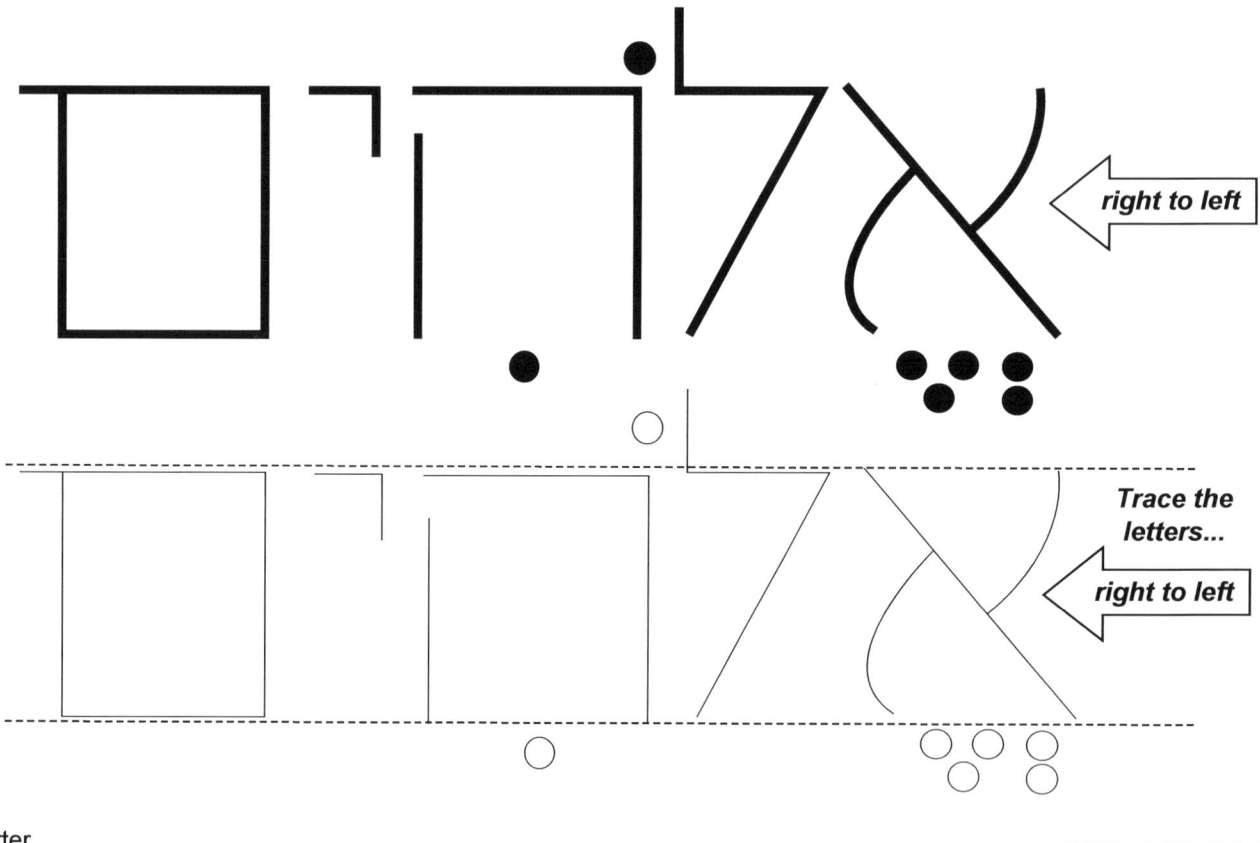

right to left

Trace the letters...
right to left

letter name:	**FINAL MAYM**	**HAY** and **CHEE-REEK MAH-LAY**	**LAH-MED** and **CHOLAM**	**AH-LEHF** and **SH'VAH-SEH-GOL**	*right to left, from top to bottom*
consonant sound:	M	H	L	(silent)	*right to left, from top to bottom*
vowel sound:		ee	oh	eh	

transliteration (left to right): **eh-lo-HEEM**

English translation: **divine one, God, gods, superhuman beings** (including **angels**), **judges** or **rulers** (in the sense of carrying out divine will or having great power). Strong's #430. NOTE: This noun, Elohim, is actually a plural noun, but is frequently used in scripture to refer to the One God who created all and is over all. This same exact word is used in scripture to mean "gods", plural. Translators must choose the correct meaning by context.

Pronouns: Singular and Plural

Pronouns can have three attributes: **Person, Gender and Number.**

We've discussed **gender** in previous lessons. Almost every pronoun will have either masculine or feminine gender. (There are also several exceptional pronouns which can be used to refer to both a masculine and feminine subject. In those cases, we call that pronoun a "common" pronoun, because it is common to both genders.)

Number indicates whether the pronoun refers to just a single person or more than one person. If it refers to a single person or entity, we say the pronoun is "singular." If if refers to more than one person or entity, we say the pronoun is "plural."

Person describes the relationship between a subject and its verb, showing whether the subject is speaking about itself, being spoken to, or being spoken about. It may help to picture yourself talking to a friend about a secret surprise party for another friend. Here is something that you might say:

I was wondering if **you** would like to order the cake. **She** really likes chocolate.
❶ ❷ ❸

In the above example, notice how the numbers proceed in order, from the person speaking **about himself/herself** (1st person), to the person **being spoken to** (2nd person), and lastly the person **being spoken about** (3rd person).

The above example happens to use all singular subjects. It's an example of one person talking to another person about yet another person. What would it be like if all the pronouns were plural, though? For example, what if you and your spouse wanted to talk to your Bible study group about a surprise party for your rabbi's entire family? Then this is how the sentences would change:

We were wondering if some of **you** would like to order the cake. **They** really like chocolate.
❶ ❷ ❸

Interestingly, the same rules apply regarding "person." The "1st person" still refers to the people talking **about themselves**, the "2nd person" still refers to the people **being spoken to**, and the "3rd person" still refers to the **people being spoken about.** The only difference is that the singular pronouns all become plural.

On the following page we have provided all the pronouns in Hebrew which are used in the subject of a sentence. We have listed the singular pronouns on the right, and the plural pronouns on the left. Some of them you will recognize from previous lessons.

Also, we have included a 3-part code next to each pronoun: a numerical digit followed by two letters. The numerical digit represents the **person** (1-1st, 2-2nd or 3-3rd); the next letter represents the **gender** (M-masculine, F-feminine or C-common); and the last letter represents the **number** (S-singular, P-plural).

Plural Pronouns | Singular Pronouns

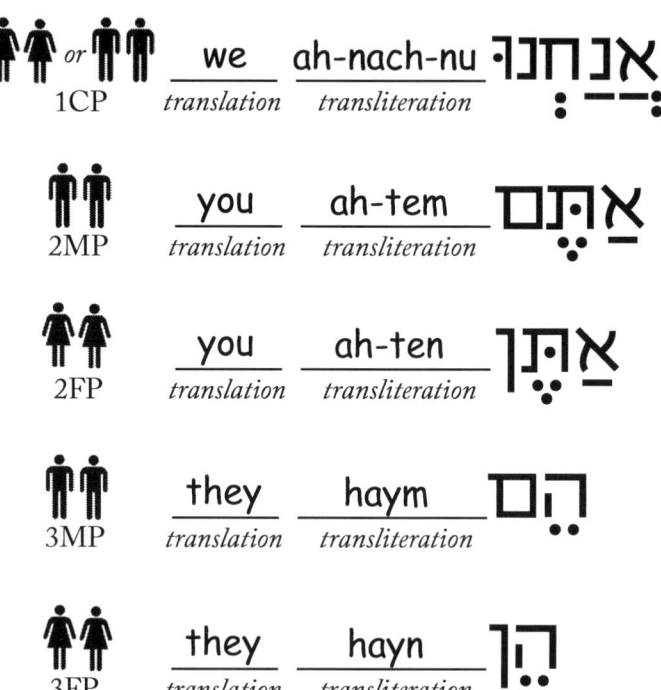
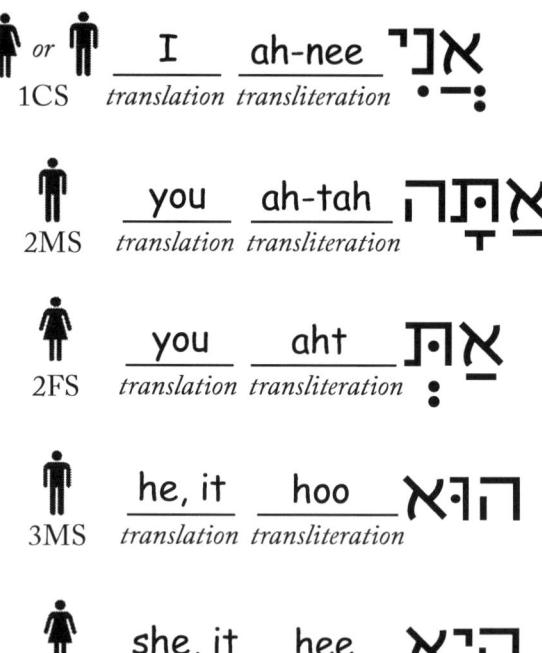

One other thing: You may have noticed that the list above doesn't mention a "mixed group" of males and females. In the case of mixed groups, Hebrew simply uses the masculine plural form.

Exercise: The list below is a duplicate of the list above, but with the transliteration and translation missing. Cover up the top half of this page and try to fill in as much as possible from memory. You can peek as much as you need to. Practice memorizing the person, gender and number of each form.

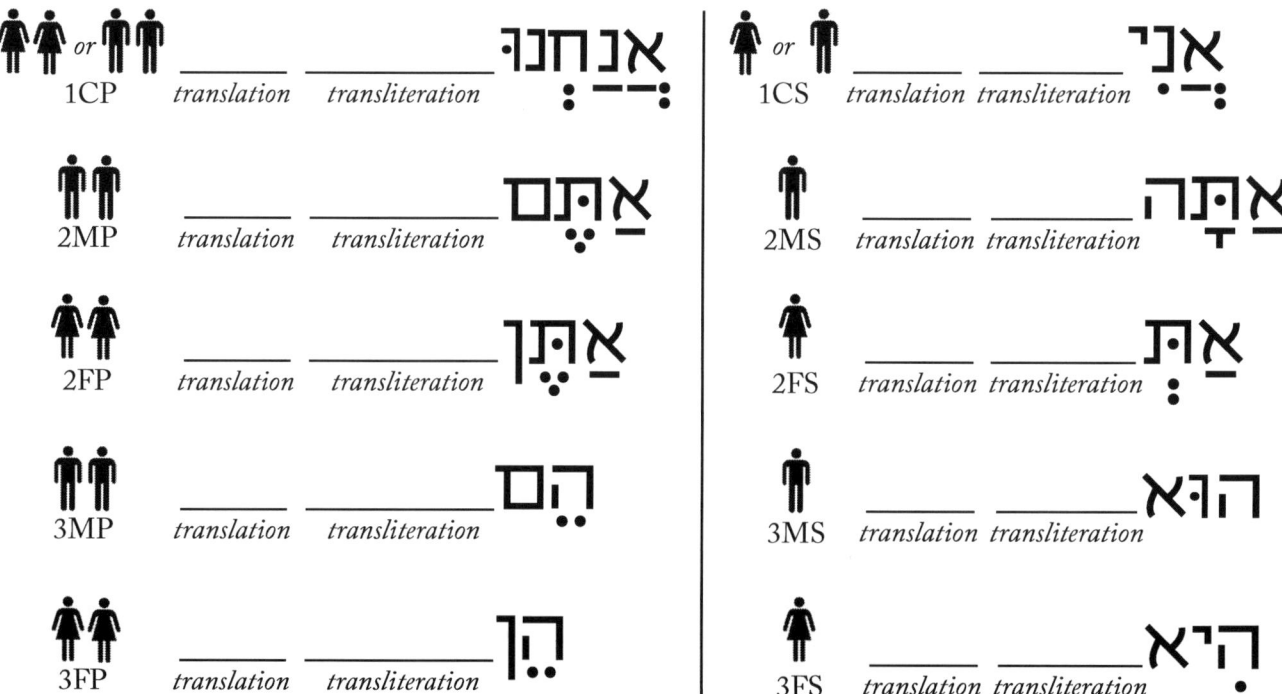

HEBREW NUGGETS

HOW MUCH BETTER IT IS TO GET WISDOM THAN GOLD!
AND TO GET UNDERSTANDING IS TO BE CHOSEN ABOVE SILVER.
Proverbs 16:16

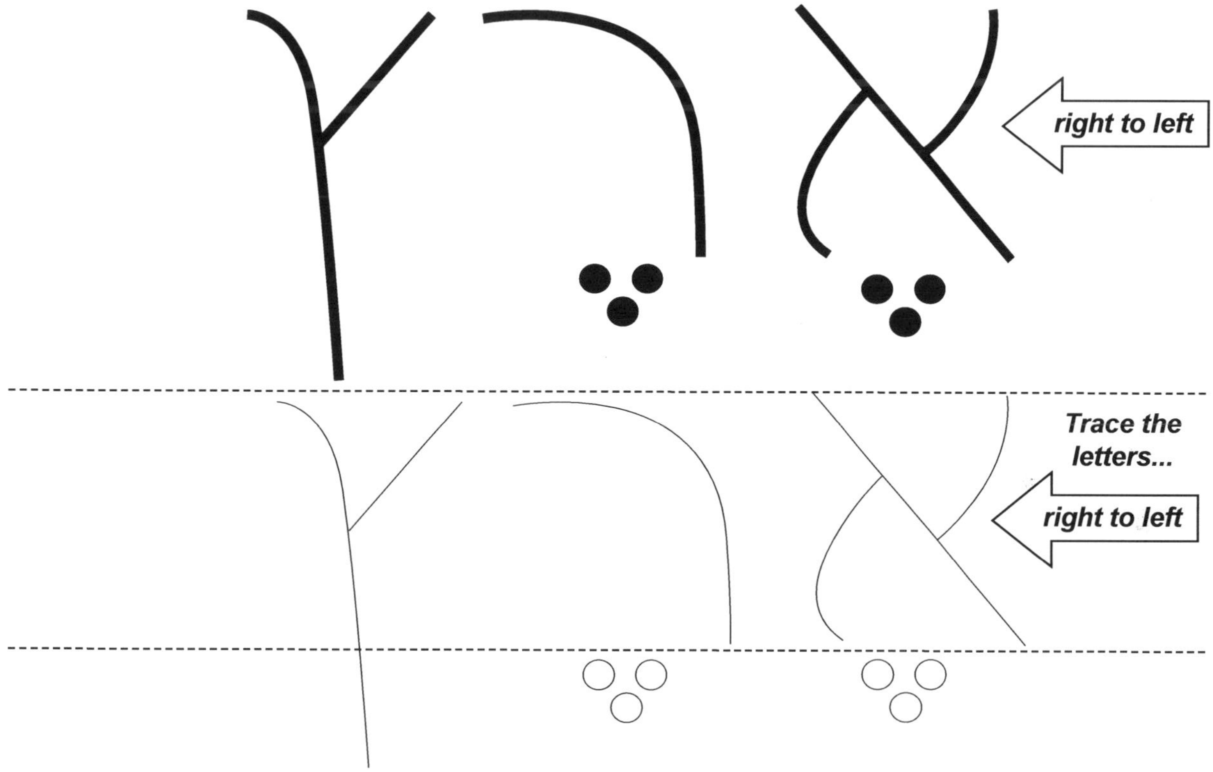

right to left

Trace the letters...
right to left

letter name:	**FINAL TSAH-DEE**	**RAYSH** and **SEH-GOL**	**AH-LEHF** and **SEH-GOL**	*right to left, from top to bottom*
vowel name:				
consonant sound:	**TS**	**R**	**(silent)**	*right to left, from top to bottom*
vowel sound:		eh	eh	

transliteration (left to right): **EH-rets**

English translation: **earth, land, country and its land, region,** as in the phrase "EH-rets yis-rah-ayl" - "the land of Israel."   Strong's #776; 2,503 occurrences in the TaNaCH (Old Testament Hebrew scriptures).

About Book Type

Some of you are probably itching to get into some real books that contain Hebrew, be they your *Strong's Concordance** or your *TaNaCH*.** Either way, you're going to want to learn how to recognize all the Hebrew letters in **"book type."**

You've probably noticed the "book type" column by now on your Cheat Sheet. In most cases, the letters are not too different looking from the hand-drawn letters you have been writing. They just look a little fancier, having "serifs," or flourishes, here and there. In most cases, they just look a little thicker in certain places, like calligraphy does.

To help you get familiar with **book type**, we have included some flashcards on the next several pages. Tear them out carefully and cut them on the lines. The front of each card has the Hebrew letter in **book type;** the back has the letter name and its pronunciation. Enjoy practicing with *yet another set of flashcards.* (It might be time to invest in a small wagon, just for toting all your sets of flashcards around!)

* *Strong's Concordance and Dictionary* - a popular Bible study tool that lists all the occurrences of the King James English words in the Bible, with their scripture references, along with a Hebrew and Greek Dictionary.

** *TaNaCH* - an abbreviation for Torah, N'viim and K'tuvim (Law, Prophets and Writings), i.e., the Old Testament in its original Hebrew language.

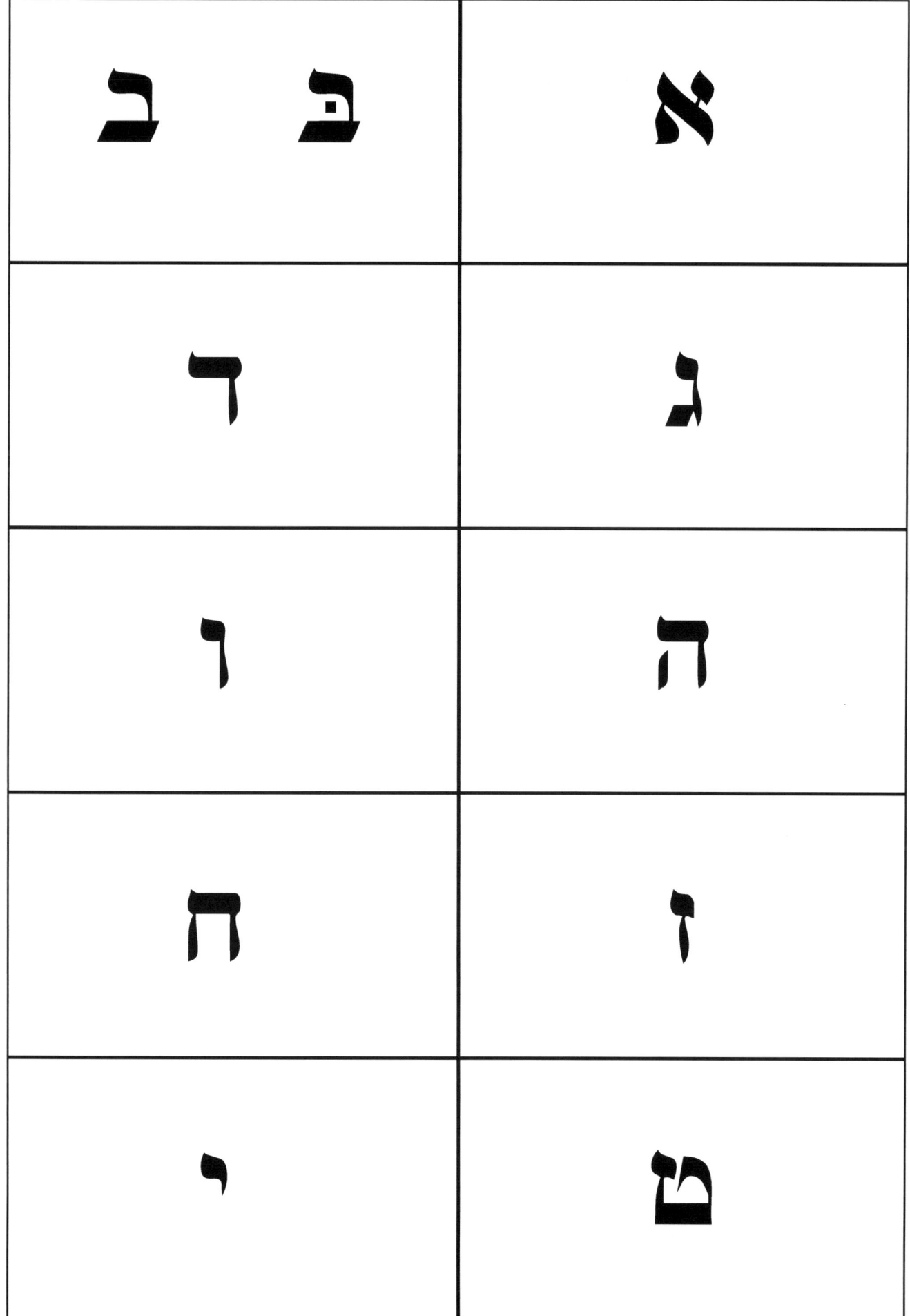

Name: Ah-lehf **Pronounced:** (silent)	**Name: Bayt or Vayt** **Pronounced:** B as in Boy or V as in Vase
Name: Gimel **Pronounced:** G as in Girl	**Name: Dah-let** **Pronounced:** D as in Door
Name: Hay **Pronounced:** H as in Hay	**Name: Vav** **Pronounced:** V as in Vase
Name: Zah-yin **Pronounced:** Z as in Zoo	**Name: Chayt** **Pronounced:** Ch as in Bach
Name: Tayt **Pronounced:** T as in Toe	**Name: Yōd or Yood** **Pronounced:** Y as in Yarn

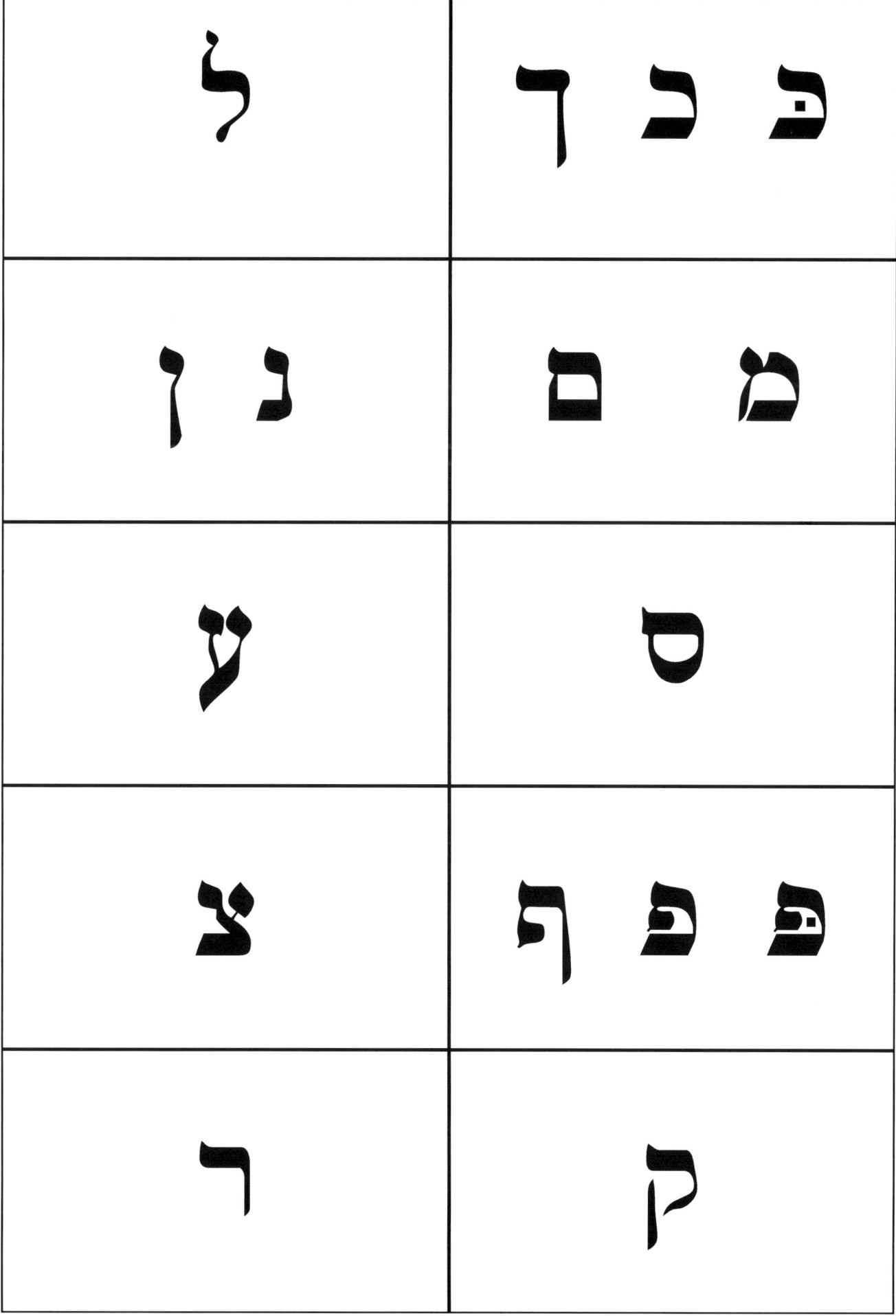

Name: Kaf or Chaf **Pronounced:** K as in Kite Ch as in Bach	**Name: Lah-med** **Pronounced:** L as in Light
Name: Maym **Pronounced:** M as in Mom	**Name: Noon** **Pronounced:** N as in Nose
Name: Sah-mech **Pronounced:** S as in Soup	**Name: Ah-yin** **Pronounced:** (Silent)
Name: Pay or Fay **Pronounced:** P as in Pad or F as in Food	**Name: Tsah-dee** **Pronounced:** Ts as in Cats
Name: Kōf **Pronounced:** K as in Kite	**Name: Raysh** **Pronounced:** R as in Rope

שׁ שִׁ	ת תִ

Name: Sheen or Seen Pronounced: SH as in Ship or S as in Soup	Name: Tahv Pronounced: T as in Top

The Furtive Patach

You'll recall from all our previous lessons that the correct order in which we sound out any Hebrew syllable is to *first* pronounce the consonant, *then* the vowel below it or after it. We pronounce from *right to left, top to bottom*. This general rule is illustrated in the syllable divisions of the now familiar word *Elohim* below:

heem   lo   eh

The first syllable **begins** with a "silent" consonant, then is **followed** by the "eh" vowel sound.
The second syllable **begins** with the "L" consonant, then is **followed** by the "oh" vowel sound.
The third syllable **begins** with the "H" consonant, then is **followed** by the "ee" vowel sound...
    then is completed with the final "M" consonant since there are no remaining sounds.

You see the pattern: consonant, then vowel. Top, then bottom. This is the general rule of Hebrew pronunciation, but we have to say "general" because there is an exception to this rule: **"the furtive patach."** "Furtive" means "sly", "thieving" or "shifty", and you'll see why in a moment.

The **furtive patach exception** goes as follows: Whenever a Hebrew word ends in the letter Chayt ח or a dotted Hey ה and has a patach vowel mark under that letter, we FIRST pronounce the vowel sound and THEN add the consonant sound! It's as though the "shifty" patach steals the position of the consonant, cutting ahead in line to be first. **Here's a famous example. Try to pronounce this word.**

Strong's #7307
Noun, Fem.

If you guessed "roo-chah", that was a good guess! But, surprise! **The pronunciation is actually "roo-ach."** This is because the furtive patach exception is in effect. Whenever you see a Chayt at the end of a word having a patach under it, **you're supposed to say "ach", not "chah."** Also, you'll place the accent on the syllable before. (By the way, this word means "wind" or "spirit," as in *Ruach ha Kodesh*, The Holy Spirit.)

Exercise: Transliterate the following Biblical words which contain the furtive patach:

translation: "Anointed One"
Noun, Masc., Strong's #4899   _____   משיח ❶
                                  transliteration

translation: "Noah"
Prop. Name, Masc., Strong's #5146   _____   נח ❷
                                        transliteration

translation: "glad, merry, joyful"
Adjective., Strong's #8056   _____   שמח ❸
                                 transliteration

translation: "altar"
Noun, Masc., Strong's #4196   _____   מזבח ❹
                                  transliteration

translation: "ability, strength"
Noun, Masc., Strong's #3581   _____   כח ❺
                                  transliteration

Messiah's Alphabet Book 1 | Page 57

The Furtive Patach

ANSWER KEY

translation: "Anointed One" Noun, Masc., Strong's #4899	mah-SHEE-ach *transliteration*	מָשִׁיחַ	**1**
translation: "Noah" Prop. Name, Masc., Strong's #5146	NO-ach *transliteration*	נֹחַ	**2**
translation: "glad, merry, joyful" Adjective., Strong's #8056	sah-MAY-ach *transliteration*	שָׂמֵחַ	**3**
translation: "altar" Noun, Masc., Strong's #4196	miz-BAY-ach *transliteration*	מִזְבֵּחַ	**4**
translation: "ability, strength" Noun, Masc., Strong's #3581	KO-ach *transliteration*	כֹּחַ	**5**

What the heck is a patach?

Note: The Furtive Patach is not to be confused with Freddie Patek, the former major league baseball shortstop.

HEBREW NUGGETS

HOW MUCH BETTER IT IS TO GET WISDOM THAN GOLD!
AND TO GET UNDERSTANDING IS TO BE CHOSEN ABOVE SILVER.

Proverbs 16:16

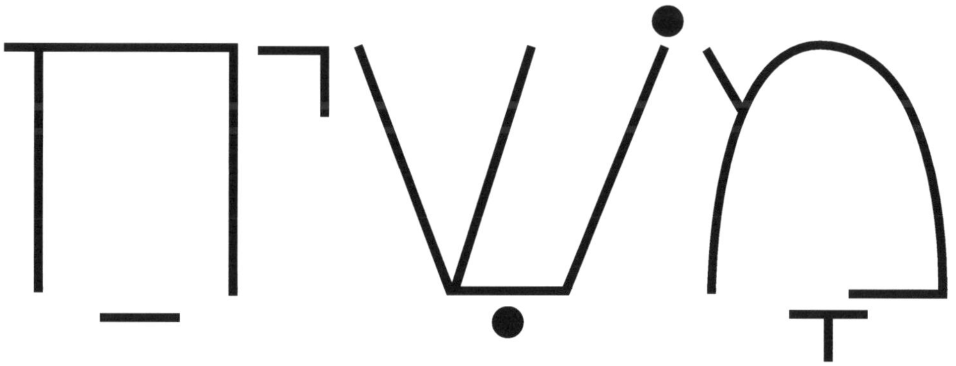

מָשִׁיחַ ← *right to left*

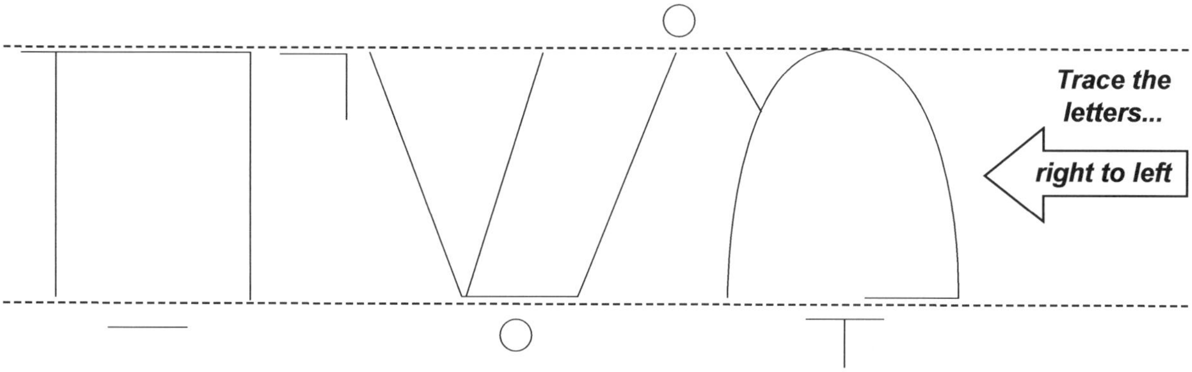

מָשִׁיחַ ← *Trace the letters... right to left*

letter name: vowel name:	**CHAYT** and **FURTIVE PAH-TACH**	**SHEEN** and **CHEE-REEK MAH-LAY**	**MAYM** and **KAH-MATS**	*right to left, from top to bottom*
consonant sound: vowel sound:	(ach)	SH ee	M ăh	*right to left, from top to bottom*

transliteration (left to right): **mah-SHEE-ach**

English translation: **anointed (anointed one), Messiah** (from *mashach*, verb: to smear, wipe, stroke with the finger as with oil; to anoint). Translated from Greek into English as "Christ". Strong's #4899.

Messiah's Alphabet Book 1 | Page 59

HEBREW NUGGETS

HOW MUCH BETTER IT IS TO GET WISDOM THAN GOLD!
AND TO GET UNDERSTANDING IS TO BE CHOSEN ABOVE SILVER.

Proverbs 16:16

⇦ *right to left*

Trace the letters...
⇦ *right to left*

letter name:	**CHAYT and**		**RAYSH**	*right to left, from top to bottom*
vowel name:	**FURTIVE PATACH**	**SHOO-ROOK**		
consonant sound:	**(ach)**		**R**	*right to left, from top to bottom*
vowel sound:		**oo**		

transliteration (left to right): **ROO-ach**

English translation: **breath, wind, spirit.** As in *Ruach Ha Kodesh*, The Holy Spirit. Also translated: **mind, motives, thoughts, blast, anger, wrath.** Strong's #7307; 377 occurrences in the TaNaCH (Old Testament Hebrew scriptures).

Simple Sentences Using Pronouns and the "Top Ten" Nouns

In the "word bank" below, we have listed the top ten most commonly found nouns in the Hebrew Old Testament (TaNaCH), along with all the pronouns you learned in previous lessons. The number of times each Hebrew word occurs in the TaNaCH, in this form or a variant/plural spelling, is listed next to each entry in the list. *Note: the little accent mark < above certain words has been added to indicate which syllable should be stressed, and is not actually a part of the Hebrew spelling. Where no accent mark is present, stress the last syllable.*

After learning all the words on this page, you will be able to recognize **29,313** of the words in the Hebrew scriptures! There are 419,687 total words in the Hebrew scriptures, so that means after memorizing this lesson you will be able to recognize **7%** of the words in the TaNaCH. That's an incredible return for memorizing one worksheet containing only ten pronouns and ten nouns!

Exercise: Transliterate and translate the following sentences.

1. אֲנִי מֶלֶךְ.
2. אַתָּה אִישׁ.
3. הִיא אֶרֶץ.
4. הֵם אֱלֹהִים.
5. הוּא אֱלֹהִים.

Messiah's Alphabet Book 1 | Page 61

Simple Sentences Using Pronouns and the "Top Ten" Nouns

ANSWER KEY

I am a king. *translation*	ah-nee meh-lech *transliteration*	אֲנִי מֶלֶךְ. ❶
You are a man. *translation*	ah-tah eesh *transliteration*	אַתָּה אִישׁ. ❷
It is a land. *translation*	hee eh-retz *transliteration*	הִיא אֶרֶץ. ❸
They are gods. *translation*	haym eh-lo-heem *transliteration*	הֵם אֱלֹהִים. ❹
He is G-d. *translation*	hoo eh-lo-heem *transliteration*	הוּא אֱלֹהִים. ❺

Write Your Own Simple Sentences Using Pronouns and the "Top Ten" Nouns

Exercise: Translate each of the English sentences below into Hebrew. Be careful to match the genders and numbers of each pronoun and noun. Use the word bank above for reference.

1 It is a house. _____

2 It is a hand. _____

3 It is a land. _____

4 You are God. _____

5 We are a people. _____

6 It is a day. _____

7 You are a son. _____

Write Your Own Simple Sentences Using Pronouns and the "Top Ten" Nouns

ANSWER KEY

1 It is a house. הוּא בַּיִת.

2 It is a hand. הִיא יָד.

3 It is a land. הִיא אֶרֶץ.

4 You are God. אַתָּה אֱלֹהִים.

5 We are a people. אֲנַחְנוּ עַם.

6 It is a day. הוּא יוֹם.

7 You are a son. אַתָּה בֵּן.

The Definite Article

In English, we have parts of speech called "articles" which are placed before nouns. There are two types of articles: **indefinite** ("a" or "an"); and **definite** ("the"). The indefinite articles "a" or "an" imply the speaker **does not know, or is not attempting to indicate,** the exact identity to which the noun refers. The definite article "the" implies the speaker or writer **"definitely" knows, or "definitely" is attempting to indicate,** the exact identity to which the noun refers. Here are some English examples of the indefinite and definite article:

1. Police say the man may be hiding in <u>a</u> house on the south side of the city. *(indefinite)*

2. This is <u>the</u> house my father built with his own hands. *(definite)*

In the first sentence, the speaker wasn't "definite" about which house the man was hiding in, so he used the indefinite article "<u>a</u>". In the second sentence, the speaker was "definite" about which house he was referring to, so he used the definite article "<u>the</u>."

In Hebrew, there is no indefinite article. If you come across a sentence such as the following, you are expected to insert the words "<u>a</u>" or "<u>an</u>" as necessary.

I am a king. אֲנִי מֶלֶךְ
                        (king) *(I)*

Hebrew does have a definite article, pronounced "ha." Interestingly, **it is not a separate word.** Instead, the letter *hey* (ה) is attached to the beginning of the Hebrew noun as a **prefix**. Usually, the vowel *patach* (—) will be under the ה. Also, a dot is sometimes added inside the letter following the ה.

I am the king. אֲנִי הַמֶּלֶךְ
                    (the king) *(I)*

Note, in this case, the dot added to the letter *maym* מ in the word *melech*.

Sometimes, instead of a *patach* (—), a *kamatz* (ָ) or a *seh-gol* (ֶ) might be used under the ה.

The **vowels of some words might also change slightly** when the definite article ה is added.

Don't be overly concerned if you see these changes in vowels or added dots; they are simply spelling changes. No one expects beginners in Hebrew to keep track of them. **All you have to do is recognize the basic consonants of the word, pronounce the vowels however you see them spelled, and realize that a ה in front of a word means "the."** Just for fun, though, see if you can spot any spelling changes in the following exercises.

Transliterate and translate the following sentences.

                 MS   3MS

1. הוּא בַּיִת.

translation   _transliteration_

הוּא הַבַּיִת.

translation   _transliteration_

                 MS   2MS

2. אַתָּה בֵּן.

translation   _transliteration_

אַתָּה הַבֵּן.

translation   _transliteration_

                 MS   2MS

3. אַתָּה אִישׁ.

translation   _transliteration_

אַתָּה הָאִישׁ.

translation   _transliteration_

                 FS   3FS

4. הִיא אֶרֶץ.

translation   _transliteration_

הִיא הָאָרֶץ.

translation   _transliteration_

ANSWER KEY

1. הוּא בַּיִת. — hoo BAH-yit. — It is a house.

הוּא הַבַּיִת. — hoo ha-BAH-yit. — It is the house.

2. אַתָּה בֵּן. — atah bayn. — You are a son.

אַתָּה הַבֵּן. — atah ha-bayn. — You are the son.

3. אַתָּה אִישׁ. — atah eesh. — You are a man.

אַתָּה הָאִישׁ. — atah ha-eesh. — You are the man.

4. הִיא אֶרֶץ. — hee EH-rets. — It is a land.

הִיא הָאָרֶץ. — hee ha-AH-rets. — It is the land.

HEBREW NUGGETS

HOW MUCH BETTER IT IS TO GET WISDOM THAN GOLD!
AND TO GET UNDERSTANDING IS TO BE CHOSEN ABOVE SILVER.
Proverbs 16:16

אֶחָד

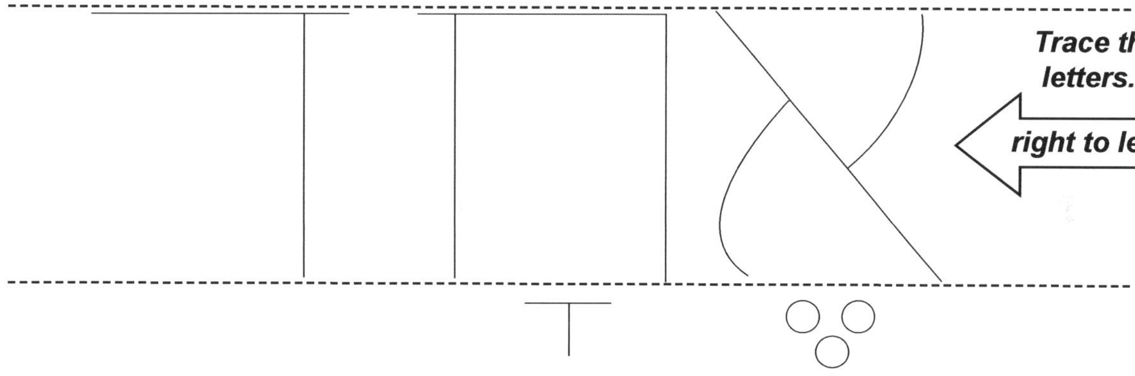

Trace the letters...
right to left

letter name:	**DAH-LET**	**CHAYT** and **KAH-MATZ**	**AH-LEHF** and **SEH-GOL**	*right to left, from top to bottom*
vowel name:				
consonant sound:	D	CH	(silent)	*right to left, from top to bottom*
vowel sound:		ah	eh	

transliteration (left to right): **eh-CHAD**

English translation: **one** (*a numeral, often translated as an adjective: "one" or "united"*). May be a singular entity, "one", or a "unity" comprised of two or more entities in combination. Used in "The LORD is one," Deut. 6:4 (from the liturgy "The Sh'ma").   Strong's #259; 967 occurrences in the TaNaCH (Old Testament Hebrew scriptures).

Messiah's Alphabet Book 1 | Page 67

The Double-Duty Dot

Sometimes words in Hebrew can be spelled in more than one way, and both ways are correct.

In English, we have many such examples, called **variant spellings:**

Aesthetic / Esthetic
Advisor / Adviser
Axe / Ax
Barbecue / Barbeque
Gray / Grey
Theater / Theatre
Collectable / Collectible

In each case, whatever spelling the writer prefers may be used as desired. The same situation occurs in Hebrew. One place we see variant spellings is when the vowel **cholam appears without its usual vav**, appearing as simply a dot floating above the word. The best known example of this is in the Hebrew word peace (*shalom*):

In both spellings above, the word is pronounced identically, *shalom*, and means the exact same thing. It is, in fact, the same word, but with **variant spellings.**

There are times, however, when the dot which represents the "o" sound of the cholam above will play two roles simultaneously. For this reason, we have named it **"the double-duty dot."**

Take a look at the following word, *shalosh*, which means "three."

Here, the dot which serves as the cholam making the "o" sound is also serving as the dot on the right side of the sheen which gives us the "sh sound.

So, the dot acts as both part of the sheen and as the cholam; i.e., "double duty." Two other words, as examples, are *yoshayv* and *moshav*, below.

"settlement" מוֹשָׁב   יֹשֵׁב "he dwells"

The way to tell that a dot is truly "double duty" is by looking at the consonant before it. If you cannot find any other vowel underneath or immediately following that consonant, then the dot in question <u>must</u> be a cholam ("oh" sound), because you <u>must</u> pronounce some kind of vowel sound in every syllable.

The Double Sehgolet

People who only know enough Hebrew to be dangerous will often tell you widely-believed, yet false, generalizations about the language. One we hear frequently is "you should always put the accent on the last syllable" of multi-syllable words. This is certainly not the case for Hebrew words with more than two syllables, and, although most two-syllable words are accented on the last syllable, there are many exceptions. The most common exception is the **"double sehgolet"** rule (pronounced "seh-GO-let").

More often than not, a two-syllable word is pronounced with emphasis on the *last* syllable, as in this word, *shah-BAHT*:

שַׁבָּת [accent]

However, if a word contains two consecutive seh-gol vowels (ֶ ֶ), then the emphasis is placed on the syllable containing the FIRST seh-gol. The following word is pronounced **MEH-lech,** not meh-LECH:

מֶלֶךְ [accent]

In short, if you see (ֶ ֶ) in any Hebrew word, emphasize the syllable containing seh-gohl #1.
              2 1

Try pronouncing the following words which are "double sehgolet" examples:

הַשֶּׁמֶשׁ   חֶדֶר   עֶרֶב

ha-SHEH-mesh   CHEH-dehr   EH-rev
the sun   *room*   *evening*

Let's Read Scripture

The goal of this book has been to help you learn to read, write, speak and understand some basic words of Biblical Hebrew. We thought it would be fitting to close with a short reading from scripture, known within Judaism as "The Sh'ma." The first word of Deuteronomy 6:4 is "Sh'ma", which means to "heed," or "to hear with an obedient spirit."

The Sh'ma is the most well-known prayer, or statement of faith, within Judaism. **It has been considered the primary fundamental statement in Judaism since before the time of Yeshua.** It is a direct quote of Deuteronomy 6:4, in which God states His commandments to His people Israel through His prophet, Moses. The Sh'ma commands: "Hear, O Israel, the Lord our God, the Lord is one."

The Sh'ma is the first commandment in Deuteronomy 6:4, then *followed* in Deut. 6:5 by a *second* part: **"and you shall love** (in Hebrew, *v'ahavta*) the Lord your God with all your heart, all your soul and all your strength." In Mark 12:29, when was asked **which was the most important commandment,** Yeshua's answer was to quote the **Sh'ma:** "The most important one is this: Hear, O Israel, the Lord our God, the Lord is one." He then continued with the "V'ahavta": the commandment beginning with "and you shall love." The scribe who had posed the question replied, "Well said, teacher." The well-known "statement of faith" of the Sh'ma was received unquestioningly by the scribe and the crowd, who all knew it by heart. Yeshua's teaching was simply expounding on the Sh'ma, expressing the original intent and spirit of this fundamental commandment.

Let's take a moment to thank our Lord for permitting us to reach this point in our studies, in which we are now able to read His very words in His holy language. Enjoy pronouncing the Hebrew of the scripture below.

שְׁמַע	יִשְׂרָאֵל	יְיָ	אֱלֹהֵינוּ	יְיָ	אֶחָד.
sh'MA	yis-ra-AYL	abbreviation for יהוה #3068 (God's holy, personal name, not pronounced*)	eh-lo-HAY-nu #430 "our God"	abbreviation for יהוה #3068 (God's holy, personal name, not pronounced*)	eh-CHAD #259 "one"
#8085 "Heed, listen!"	#3478 "Israel"				

*These abbreviations are not intended to be pronounced out loud (they wouldn't actually mean anything to a Hebrew speaker if you tried to say them out loud to him/her). They are just a visual symbol, a substitution, reminding the reader that these spots are where the name of God appears in the actual Hebrew scriptures. (This is similar to our "&" symbol in English, substituting for the word "and." We know we are supposed to pronounce the word "and" whenever we see the "&" symbol.) So, what *do* people say when they are reading out loud and come across these abbreviations? Many Jewish people will say "Adonai." Some will say "HaShem", meaning "The Name." Christian and Jewish translators alike have traditionally used the word "Lord" (usually typeset in "small caps" as shown here) as a substitute for God's personal name in Bible translation. All three show respect for the holiness of God's personal name.

For Further Study

Would you like to continue in your study of Biblical Hebrew? Here is a list of books we have found very helpful once you have mastered *Messiah's Alphabet Book 1*:

Messiah's Alphabet Book 2: Building a Biblical Vocabulary
by James T. and Lisa M. Cummins
Continue to build your Biblical vocabulary and grammar skills with the next book in the *Messiah's Alphabet* series. This book reviews all the grammar and vocabulary from Book 1, then teaches the conjunction "and", plus plural nouns, adjectives, and possessives for singular nouns. The easy-going, fun approach of Book 1 continues in this book with puzzles, songs, games, cartoons and more. All answers provided with the exercises. Audio for all vocabulary introduced in the book is available. (More books by James and Lisa Cummins are shown on the following pages.)

The Interlinear Bible: Hebrew-Greek-English
Hendrickson Publishing
This is the only complete interlinear Bible available in English - and it's keyed to Strong's "Exhaustive Concordance." *The Interlinear Bible* is a time-saving tool for researching the subtle nuances and layers of meaning within the original Biblical languages. Featuring the complete Hebrew and Greek texts with a direct English rendering below each word, it also includes "The Literal Translation of the Bible" in the outside column. Strong's numbers are printed directly above the Hebrew and Greek words. Strong's numbers enable even those with no prior knowledge of Greek or Hebrew to easily access a wealth of language reference works keyed to Strong's – Greek/Hebrew dictionaries, analytical lexicons, concordances, word studies, Bible software and more. **Suggested**: Use this book to find Strong's numbers for any scripture in the Bible, then refer to *Strong's Exhaustive Concordance* for definitions (see next entry).

The New Strong's Expanded Exhaustive Concordance of the Bible
by James Strong; Thomas Nelson Publishing
This concordance provides exhaustive lists of all the English words found in the King James Version, each keyed to a "Strong's number" corresponding to the numbered Strong's Hebrew and Greek dictionaries (included). No knowledge of Hebrew or Greek is needed in order to look up any word in the Bible in the original languages. This particular version also contains the best of *Vine's Complete Expository Dictionary of Old and New Testament Words*. Additional cross-references from leading dictionaries make this an excellent reference tool for pastors, teachers, and all students of the Bible. **Suggested:** Use this book to understand the Hebrew or Greek meaning of *any* word in your Bible. Discover its true, full meaning in the original languages.

Other Books
by James T. and Lisa M. Cummins

Messiah's Alphabet Book 2: Building A Biblical Vocabulary follows Book 1 in the *Messiah's Alphabet* series. In Book 2, you will review all the grammar and vocabulary from Book 1, then learn the conjunction "and", how to make plural nouns, adjectives, and possessives for singular nouns. The easy-going, fun approach of Book 1 continues in this book with puzzles, songs, games, cartoons and more. All answers provided with the exercises. Audio for all vocabulary available.

Available on Amazon.com

Messiah's Alphabet Book 3: More Grammar for Biblical Hebrew follows Book 2 in the *Messiah's Alphabet* grammar series. In Book 3, you will add even more Biblical Hebrew words to your vocabulary, along with other essential grammar concepts, including prepositions, participles and the "construct form" (word pairs). The fun, friendly teaching style of Books 1 and 2 will continue in this book with exercises, puzzles, games, cartoons and guided scripture readings. All answers are provided in the text. Audio files of every lesson available.

Projected release date on Amazon.com: late 2016 to early 2017

Other Books by James T. and Lisa M. Cummins, *continued*

Messiah's Alphabet: Names Have Meaning is an exploration into the actual Hebrew meanings of some of the names of people, places and objects mentioned in the Bible. Surprising discoveries will unfold as you connect the true meaning of each Hebrew name with its prophetic significance and fulfilment in scripture. The hidden Hebrew meanings underlying the names of New Testament people and places will also be brought to light. This book assumes a basic working knowledge of the vocabulary and grammar introduced in Books 1 and 2 of the *Messiah's Alphabet* series. All answers are provided in the text. Audio files of every lesson available.

Projected release date on Amazon.com: mid to late 2017

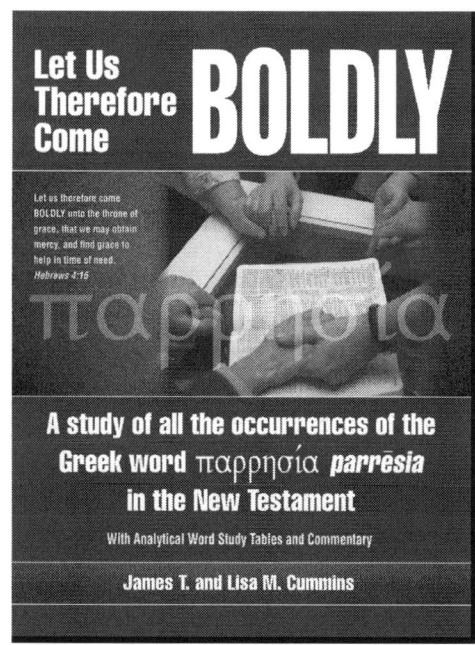

Let Us Therefore Come BOLDLY: A study of all the occurrences of the Greek word parresia *in the New Testament*

This book leads the reader through all the occurrences of the Greek word for "boldness" in the New Testament. Throughout the study, the various meanings of this deep and wonderful Greek word are uncovered, along with practical applications for the believer's life. Graphic tables and insightful commentary make it easy for the student to understand the significance of every separate mention of the Greek word *parresia* – even if the student has no knowledge of the Greek language.

Available on Amazon.com

Phrase-By-Phrase Harmony of the Gospels
Available on Amazon.com

Finally! A harmony of the gospels with all the tools you need to effectively study every phrase of the gospels in chronological order.

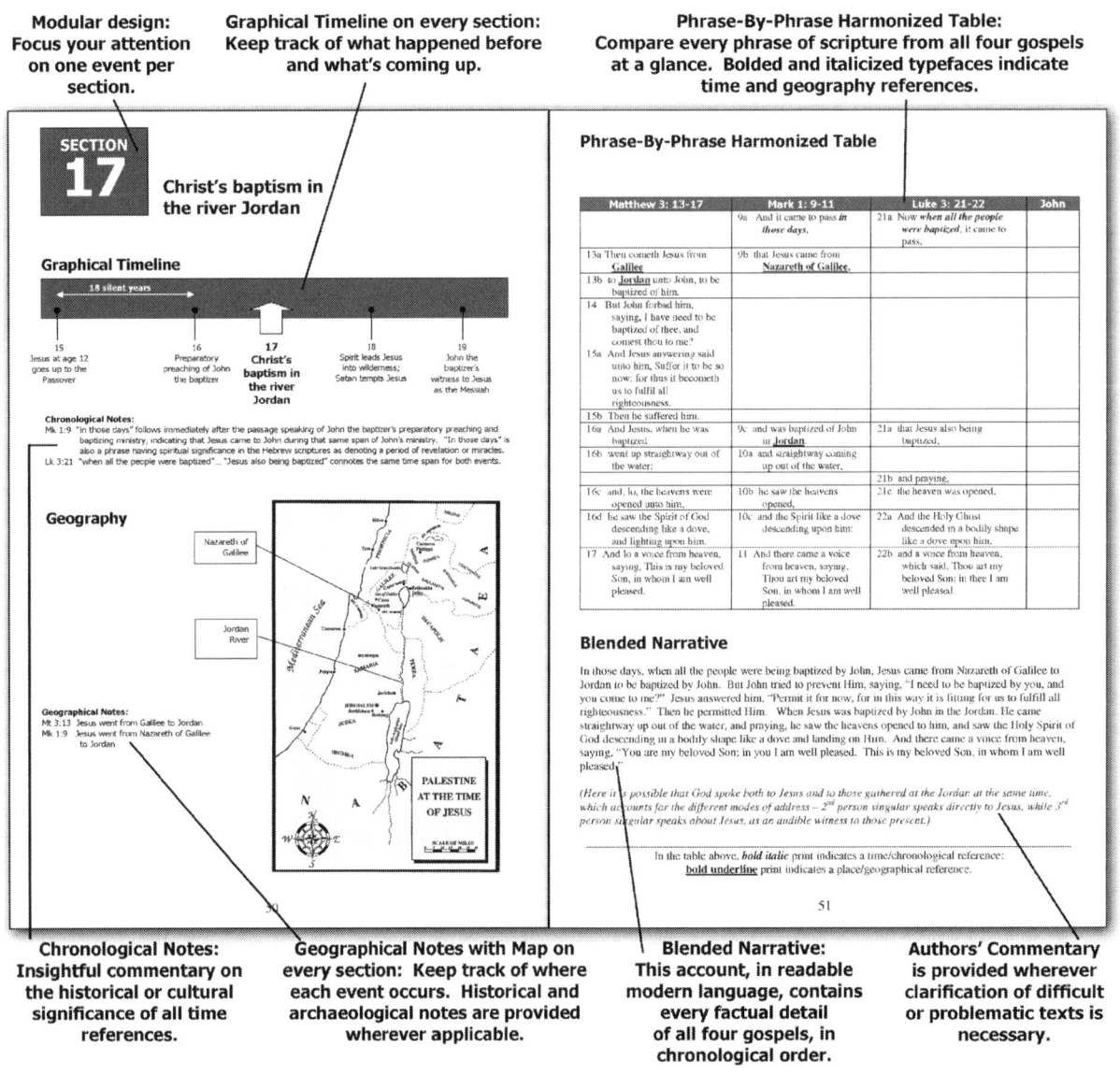

Modular design: Focus your attention on one event per section.

Graphical Timeline on every section: Keep track of what happened before and what's coming up.

Phrase-By-Phrase Harmonized Table: Compare every phrase of scripture from all four gospels at a glance. Bolded and italicized typefaces indicate time and geography references.

Chronological Notes: Insightful commentary on the historical or cultural significance of all time references.

Geographical Notes with Map on every section: Keep track of where each event occurs. Historical and archaeological notes are provided wherever applicable.

Blended Narrative: This account, in readable modern language, contains every factual detail of all four gospels, in chronological order.

Authors' Commentary is provided wherever clarification of difficult or problematic texts is necessary.

The *Phrase-By-Phrase Harmony of the Gospels*, building on the foundation of centuries of great Bible scholarship, is a brand new approach to studying the events of the gospels in detailed chronological order. Rather than presenting entire passages from synoptic accounts in whole paragraphs, this harmony permits the reader to compare each fact and detail side by side. With its friendly, graphical layout – beneficial for the average small group Bible study – this book is also sufficiently technical for use as a supplemental reference in any college-level course on the gospels. The *Phrase-By-Phrase Harmony* is a versatile tool: a handy reference for pastors and teachers, or a devotional guide in daily Bible reading.

Messiah's Alphabet Book 1 | Page 74

Printed in Great Britain
by Amazon